BUT GOD!

BUT GOD!

The author of these lessons is the President of Wheaton College in Wheaton, Illinois, an office which he has held since 1940. From high school he enlisted in the Army and served in the Twenty-eighth Infantry of the famous First Division in France and Germany in the First World War. He completed his undergraduate studies at Boston University, and was a missionary for some years among the Quichua Indians of Ecuador. Forced to come home because of continued illness in the tropics, he completed his graduate work for the M.A. and Ph.D. degrees at Clark University in Worcester, Massachusetts. He taught history and political science at Wheaton for four years before being asked to accept the presidency.

His other books include: *They Found the Secret*
Out of My Life
The Disciplines of Life
The Delights of Life
Sweeter Than Honey
Just Why?
He Leadeth Me
Storms and Starlight
In Quietness and Confidence
Great Is Thy Faithfulness
Not Ashamed
Fear Not
Wiser Than They Thought
Finney Lives On
Light in Dark Ages
Then and There

BUT GOD!

Little lessons of large importance
learned from the Holy Scriptures,
with poems by Annie Johnson Flint

by

V. RAYMOND EDMAN
President, Wheaton College, Wheaton, Illinois

ZONDERVAN PUBLISHING HOUSE
GRAND RAPIDS   MICHIGAN

First printing 1962
Second printing 1963
Third printing 1964
Fourth printing . . July, 1965

Printed in the United States of America

DEDICATION

These lessons that have gone deeply into my heart are gratefully dedicated to the eye surgeons who have been used of God to preserve vision in both eyes during recent days and months of trials. They are Doctors P. Kenneth Gieser, Valdo Oleari, and Wendell Thomas of Wheaton; Faye M. Whitsell and Milton Sternberg of Chicago; Charles L. Schepens and his associates of Boston. Thank you each one, and God bless you!

Rowena Carr edited the manuscript. Typing was done by Dolores Lassen and Marjorie Frenchak. For this immeasurable help in the preparation of the manuscript, they know how grateful I am.

V.R.E.

"Westgate"
Wheaton College

ACKNOWLEDGMENTS

The scenic photos in this book were provided by the Union Pacific Railroad Company and used with its permission.

The poems of Annie Johnson Flint are copyrighted by Evangelical Publishers and are used by permission.

What Dr. Edman Says About —

What the Poet Said

But God

I know not, but God knows;
 Oh, blessed rest from fear!
All my unfolding days
 To Him are plain and clear.
Each anxious, puzzled "why?"
 From doubt or dread that grows,
Finds answer in this thought:
 I know not, but He knows.

I cannot, but God can;
 Oh, balm for all my care!
The burden that I drop
 His hand will lift and bear.
Though eagle pinions tire,
 I walk where once I ran,
This is my strength to know
 I cannot, but He can.

I see not, but God sees;
 Oh, all sufficient light!
My dark and hidden way
 To Him is always bright.
My strained and peering eyes
 May close in restful ease,
And I in peace may sleep;
 I see not, but He sees.

— ANNIE JOHNSON FLINT

1.

BUT

"But" is a conjunction *with a difference!*

"And" is likewise a conjunction, *but* it does not carry the same impact as "but." To say "and" is to give additional information which may be either trivial or tremendous; however the intent of the statement is quite complete without that which follows the conjunction. "But" is always of the contrary opinion. Not only does it add additional information but it also changes the impression and impact given by that which precedes its use. It qualifies, alters, and not infrequently completely negates that which has been said.

For example, we say: "That is a good idea, *but* . . .!" Chances are that the proposed idea will be abandoned altogether. "He is a good businessman, *but* . . ." We hear, and we hesitate to put confidence in his judgment or to invest in his business. Someone says, "She is a good friend, *but* . . ." A real friend? Hardly! The "but" keeps butting in to change the whole situation.

When the late Charles Evans Hughes, in his capacity as Secretary of State, attended a Pan-American Conference, he instructed his interpreter to give him a summarized translation of what was being spoken in Spanish or Portuguese, but he said: "While a running translation is ample for my purpose, I want you to give me every word after the speaker says *but*." What follows "but" is of the utmost importance!

In my devotional reading and study of the Bible, I

have come again and again upon the expression, "But God. . . ." Whatever may have been stated is immediately qualified, and often corrected, by that which follows "but." For example, we read in Ephesians 2:3, 4 that we "were by nature the children of wrath, even as others; *but God*, who is rich in mercy . . . ." Wicked men had their way in condemning and crucifying the Lord Jesus, "*but God* raised him from the dead" (Acts 13:30). With sighing and sorrow of heart the psalmist wrote, "My flesh and my heart faileth; *but God* is the strength of my heart, and my portion forever" (73:26). In Psalm 3:2, 3, we read that "Many there be which say of my soul, There is no help for him in God. *But thou*, O Lord, art a shield for me. . . ."

We are to be aware of that which precedes the conjunction, but after the "but" we are to believe that such promises and provision are to be appropriated by faith.

Here are some of those statements in Scripture which challenge our faith and can change the course of our life. Irrespective of what may be our circumstances and our needs, we are to remember, "*But God* . . . "!

✻   ✻   ✻   ✻

Also, here are some of Annie Johnson Flint's poems. Years ago I began to find one poem or another in a Christian periodical such as *The Sunday School Times*. Then I secured the booklets: *Songs of the Saviour, Songs of Grace and Glory, Songs of the Blessed Hope, By the Way,* and *Out of Doors*. Always I was blessed and edified by the deep spiritual truth so beautifully told in these exquisite poems. More recently I have secured her *Best Loved Poems* and Dr. Rowland V. Bingham's *Life of Annie Johnson Flint*.

I have shared the poems with many others in radio

ministry in Worcester, Massachusetts, during graduate studies at Clark University. Also I have read them again and again in the daily chapel service at Wheaton College and elsewhere, and always with blessing and helpfulness to others.

I observe that Miss Flint's poems are becoming less known in the rising generation, and that should not be. Here are some of them and you should secure all of them. A complete index is to be found in her *Life*.

This may seem to be a large recommendation — *but* you will be glad you took my suggestion.

There is that *but* again!

THY STRENGTH AND MY DAY

Give me Thy strength for my day, Lord,
    That wheresoe'er I go,
There shall no danger daunt me
    And I shall fear no foe;
So shall no task o'ercome me,
    So shall no trial fret,
So shall I walk unwearied
    The path where my feet are set;
So shall I find no burden
    Greater than I can bear,
So shall I have a courage
    Equal to all my care;
So shall no grief o'erwhelm me,
    So shall no wave o'erflow;
Give me Thy strength for my day, Lord,
    Cover my weakness so.
                    — ANNIE JOHNSON FLINT

16

2.

BUT GOD IS THE STRENGTH OF MY HEART

Truly God is good to Israel, even to such as are of a clean heart. But as for me, my feet were almost gone; my steps had well nigh slipped. For I was envious at the foolish, when I saw the prosperity of the wicked. . . . So foolish was I, and ignorant: I was as a beast before thee. Nevertheless I am continually with thee: thou hast holden me by my right hand. Thou shalt guide me with thy counsel and afterward receive me to glory. Whom have I in heaven but thee? and there is none upon earth that I desire beside thee. My flesh and my heart faileth: BUT GOD *is the strength of my heart, and my portion for ever (Psalm 73:1-3, 22-26).*

The heart is usually tougher and stronger than the flesh, because the spirit within us can rise above the infirmities of the body. In Proverbs 18:14 is the concise declaration: "The spirit of a man will sustain his infirmity; but a wounded spirit who can bear?" It is known that an athlete can continue to play in the excitement and thrill of the game even though he has suffered a broken bone. Despite multiple wounds, a soldier can continue resisting the onslaughts of the enemy. A frail girl can continue her life's calling despite appalling handicaps. But a broken heart — who then can triumph?

For the psalmist, both heart and flesh had failed. Bruised and bewildered by injustice and iniquity, he saw no prospect for the triumph of the right. He had observed the prosperity of the wicked, and therefore it seemed to him that indeed he had cleansed his heart in vain and

washed his hands in innocency. He himself had been plagued and chastened every morning while the ungodly had more than heart could wish, and in their pride they boasted: "How doth God know? and, is their knowledge in the most High?"

The psalmist found no answer to his painful dilemma until with all humility he took his case to God — "I went into the sanctuary of God; then understood I their end" (73:16, 17). When everything and everyone had failed him and injustice seemed to prevail, he found God to be his unfailing Helper: "Nevertheless I am continually with thee: thou hast holden me by my right hand. Thou shalt guide me with thy counsel, and afterward receive me to glory" (73:23, 24). And he was satisfied: "Whom have I in heaven but thee? And there is none on earth that I desire beside thee." Faith was the answer to bewilderment of heart and exhaustion of flesh.

The entire psalm hinges on the single word *but*. Up to that point there seemed to be no real help for God's troubled servant; *but God* proved Himself to be the strength of his heart and his portion forever. Then tears turned to triumph, bewilderment to blessings, and perplexity to praise.

Suppose the godless do make much gain and the impenitent are prosperous. Suppose we suffer loss because of godliness and integrity, so that poverty is our lot. God is our guide now and has prepared glory for us hereafter.

Heart would faint — but God is our strength!

Flesh would fail — but God is our portion forever!

WHAT GOD HATH PROMISED

God hath not promised
    Skies always blue,
Flower-strewn pathways
    All our lives through;
God hath not promised
    Sun without rain,
Joy without sorrow,
    Peace without pain.

But God hath promised
    Strength for the day,
Rest for the labor,
    Light for the way,
Grace for the trials,
    Help from above,
Unfailing sympathy,
    Undying love.

        — ANNIE JOHNSON FLINT

3.

BUT GOD WAS WITH JOSEPH

And Joseph was brought down to Egypt; and Potiphar, an officer of Pharaoh, captain of the guard, an Egyptian, bought him of the hands of the Ishmeelites, which had brought him down thither. And the Lord was with Joseph, and he was a prosperous man; and he was in the house of his master the Egyptian. . . . And Joseph's master took him, and put him into the prison, a place where the king's prisoners were bound: and he was there in the prison. BUT THE LORD *was with Joseph, and shewed him mercy, and gave him favour in the sight of the keeper of the prison (Genesis 39:1, 2, 20, 21).*

It seems that everyone and everything was against Joseph. His older brothers hated him and wanted to take his life; they sold him into a living death as a slave in Egypt. In Potiphar's household he was maligned and misrepresented and, consequently, cast into prison. He was an alien, a slave in a strange land, a prisoner, without a friend in the world. In that jail he could have reflected on the adversities that had brought him to that place: envy, hatred, greed, deceit, misrepresentation, ingratitude and meanness.

But the Lord was with Joseph!

Nothing or no one could deprive Joseph of that unfailing Presence. Even though life must have seemed to be without meaningful pattern or movement denoting progress toward some goal, yet Joseph could depend upon God who had made revelation to him that some day he would be in a place of pre-eminence, even over his brothers. He was in

21

God's hand, even though every man's hand was against him. God's purpose for his life would not be thwarted by man's injustice and ingratitude. The psalmist observed that God "sent a man before them, even Joseph, who was sold for a servant: whose feet they hurt with fetters: he was laid in iron: until the time that his word came: the word of the Lord tried him. The king sent and loosed him; even the ruler of the people, and let him go free" (Psalm 105: 17-20).

No one nor any circumstance can shut God out of your life if your heart is right toward Him and toward others. Like Joseph, we may be "laid in iron," but therein we will be strengthened and sweetened by the chastening of the Most High who does not fail nor forsake His own. And, since God is for us, who can be against us?

The Blessings That Remain

There are loved ones who are missing
    From the fireside and the feast;
There are faces that have vanished,
    There are voices that have ceased;
But we know they passed forever
    From our mortal grief and pain,
And we thank Thee, O our Father,
    For the blessings that remain.

Thanksgiving, oh, thanksgiving
    That their love once blessed us here,
That so long they walked beside us
    Sharing every smile and tear;
For the joy the past has brought us
    But can never take away,
For the sweet and gracious memories
    Growing dearer every day,

For the faith that keeps us patient
   Looking at the things unseen,
Knowing Spring shall follow Winter
   And the earth again be green,
For the hope of that glad meeting
   Far from mortal grief and pain —
We thank Thee, O our Father —
   For the blessings that remain.

For the love that still is left us,
   For the friends who hold us dear,
For the lives that yet may need us
   For their guidance and their cheer,
For the work that waits our doing,
   For the help we can bestow,
For the care that watches o'er us
   Wheresoe'er our steps may go,

For the simple joys of living,
   For the sunshine and the breeze,
For the beauty of the flowers
   And the laden orchard trees,
For the night and for the starlight,
   For the rainbow and the rain —
Thanksgiving, O our Father,
   For the blessings that remain.

— ANNIE JOHNSON FLINT

4

BUT GOD SHALL BE WITH YOU

And it came to pass after these things, that one told Joseph, Behold, thy father is sick: and he took with him his two sons, Manasseh and Ephraim. . . . And Israel beheld Joseph's sons, and said, Who are these? And Joseph said unto his father, They are my sons, whom God hath given me in this place. And he said, Bring them, I pray thee, unto me, and I will bless them. . . . And he blessed them that day, saying, In thee shall Israel bless, saying, God make thee as Ephraim and as Manasseh: and he set Ephraim before Manasseh. And Israel said unto Joseph, Behold, I die: BUT GOD shall be with you, and bring you again unto the land of your fathers (Genesis 48:1, 8, 9, 20, 21).

Faith in the living God is the greatest heritage.

The patriarch, Jacob, learned from his forefathers, Abraham and Isaac, to have faith in God, and when he came to die he entrusted that same heritage to his twelve sons. In particular he said these words, "But God shall be with you," to his son Joseph. The dying man had lived a long and full life, and during the many years of his earthly pilgrimage he had found the Most High God to be his unfailing helper. God had made him a wanderer in the earth that he might learn to walk with the Almighty. God had deeply tested him by sorrows and seemingly insurmountable difficulties, but through them all Jacob had found God's guidance, presence, and provision. In the deepest crisis of his walk with the Almighty, Jacob had met God face to face at Peniel. And life was forever different thereafter. So much so that even his name was changed from Jacob to Israel — "a prince with God" (Genesis 32:24-30).

Israel's most poignant sorrow was the loss of his favorite son, Joseph, whom he believed had been devoured by wild beasts. The old patriarch's joy was boundless when he learned years later that Joseph was alive and in Egypt where he had become Pharaoh's prime minister. After some years in Egypt, Israel knew that death was approaching. Above all else he wanted Joseph and all his sons to be assured that God would not fail them nor forsake them. They were in Egypt, not in the land which God had promised to them through Abraham their great-grandfather, *but God* would bring them again to the land of their fathers!

"The things which are seen are temporal," declares II Corinthians 4:18, "but the things which are not seen are eternal." Better than any material heritage that we can pass on to our children is the unwavering assurance that God will also be their God, even unto death. Wealth and health may not be their abiding portion, fortune and fame they may never have; but if only we, like Jacob, have brought them into acquaintance with the God of salvation, then they in their generation will find Him to be their unfailing Helper. They will know, as we have learned, that "he that cometh to God must believe that he is, and that he is a rewarder of them that diligently seek him" (Hebrews 11:6). They in turn, as our Lord tarries, can pass on to the following generation that same assurance.

The psalmist sang:

> Walk about Zion, and go round about her: tell the towers thereof. Mark ye well her bulwarks, consider her palaces; that ye may tell it to the generation following. For this God is our God for ever and ever: he will be our guide even unto death (Psalm 48:12-14).

We die. *But God* will be with our children!

FOUNDATION STONES

I would not lose the hard things from my life,
The rocks o'er which I stumbled long ago,
The griefs and fears, the failures and mistakes,
That tried and tested faith and patience so.

I need them now; they make the deep-laid wall,
The firm foundation-stones on which I raise —
To mount therein from stair to higher stair —
The lofty towers of my House of Praise.

Soft was the roadside turf to weary feet,
And cool the meadows where I fain had trod,
And sweet beneath the trees to lie at rest
And breathe the incense of the flower-starred sod;

But not on these might I securely build,
Nor sand nor sod withstand the earthquake shock,
I need the rough, hard boulders of the hills
To set my house on everlasting rock.

— ANNIE JOHNSON FLINT

5.

BUT GOD MEANT IT UNTO GOOD

And when Joseph's brethren saw that their father was dead, they said, Joseph will peradventure hate us, and will certainly requite us all the evil which we did unto him. And they sent a messenger unto Joseph, saying, Thy father did command before he died, saying, So shall ye say unto Joseph, Forgive, I pray thee now, the trespass of thy brethren, and their sin; for they did unto thee evil: and now, we pray thee, forgive the trespass of the servants of the God of thy father. And Joseph wept when they spake unto him. And his brethren also went and fell down before his face; and they said, Behold, we be thy servants. And Joseph said unto them, Fear not: for am I in the place of God? But as for you, ye thought evil against me; BUT GOD *meant it unto good, to bring to pass, as it is this day, to save much people alive (Genesis 50:15-20).*

The startling truth declared in Romans 8:28, "We know that all things work together for good to them that love God," was not a new revelation reserved for New Testament times. Its truth is written large throughout the Bible. Joseph's experience is an outstanding Old Testament illustration thereof. He had been envied by his brothers to the point of hatred, so much so that they sold him into slavery. More dastardly treatment can hardly be imagined. When the day came that Joseph, no longer a slave in Egypt but prime minister of the land, could help his brothers, he was only too glad so to do. They were fearful that after their father's death Joseph might change his helpfulness into hatred. Not so, Joseph sought to assure them, explaining that God meant all that had transpired to be for their good.

How can all things work together for good? The details taken separately may contain no good whatever, but *together* they are good. The late Dr. H. A. Ironside, pastor of Moody Church, was fond of telling the observation of an elderly cook at a Bible conference. She had said to the preachers, who were discussing Romans 8:28, "You all have expressed appreciation for the hot biscuits I make for you each morning. But consider — the flour itself does not taste good, nor does the baking powder, nor the shortening, nor the other ingredients; however, when I mix them all together and put them into the oven, they come out just right for biscuits. That is how I understand that God makes everything work *together* for good."

Whatever may be the circumstances of yesterday or today, they can work together for our good as long as our heart is right toward God and others. In time we can say like Joseph, *"But God* meant it unto good."

This Moment

A very present help — Psalm 46:1

He's helping me now — this moment,
  Though I may not see it or hear,
Perhaps by a friend far distant
  Perhaps by a stranger near,
Perhaps by a spoken message,
  Perhaps by the printed word;
In ways that I know and know not
  I have the help of the Lord.

He's keeping me now — this moment,
  However I need it most,
Perhaps by a single angel,
  Perhaps by a mighty host,
Perhaps by the chain that frets me,
  Or the walls that shut me in;
In ways that I know and know not,
  He keeps me from harm and sin.

He's guiding me now — this moment,
  In pathways easy or hard,
Perhaps by a door wide open,
  Perhaps by a door fast barred,
Perhaps by a joy withholden,
  Perhaps by a gladness given;
In ways that I know and know not,
  He's leading me up to heaven.

He's using me now — this moment,
  And whether I go or stand,
Perhaps by a plan accomplished,
  Perhaps when He stays my hand,
Perhaps by a word in season,
  Perhaps by a silent prayer;
In ways that I know and know not,
  His labor of love I share.

— Annie Johnson Flint

32

6

BUT GOD KNOWS THE WAY

Behold, I go forward, but he is not there: and back-ward, but I cannot perceive him: on my left hand, where he doth work, but I cannot behold him: he hideth himself on the right hand, that I cannot see him: BUT HE KNOWETH *the way that I take: when he hath tried me, I shall come forth as gold. My foot hath held his steps, his way have I kept, and not declined (Job 23:8-11).*

We are finite. God is infinite. We do not know what a day will bring forth; He knows the end from the beginning. There are times when, like Job, we seek earnestly to know the way wherein we should walk and the thing that we should do. We turn to the right hand or to the left. We go forward a bit, and then backward; but all is uncertainty, even unreality. We face fear and frustration. We discover only darkness and dismay. We hear only the echo of our own call for guidance.

We begin to appreciate quite fully the experience of the prophet Jeremiah when he declared that it is not in man to know the way that he should take. We scan carefully that promise in the first chapter of James and reread it slowly and thoughtfully: "If any of you lack wisdom, let him ask of God, that giveth to all men liberally, and upbraideth not; and it shall be given him. But let him ask in faith, nothing wavering. For he that wavereth is like a wave of the sea driven with the wind and tossed. For let not that man think that he shall receive any thing of the Lord. A double minded man is unstable in all his ways" (James 1:5-8). Then sud-

denly we become aware that we are indeed like the wave of the sea, surging upward for a brief moment or two, then sinking downward into the trough of despair. We need stability, strength, faith, faithfulness, confidence, and courage, and these we do not have.

But God knows the way that we take. It may be dark, but nothing is hidden to Him with whom light and darkness are both alike. It may be difficult, but He is never dismayed. It may be a long, never-ending way with no apparent turning, demanding a patient plodding onward, but He never grows weary. He takes the *twenty*-second mile with us, not the second only. The way may be lonely, but there is always the loveliness of His presence, whether discerned at the given moment or not.

Someday all the way will become meaningful. Life's road itself may never have changed appreciably but we shall have been transformed inwardly by our walking onward by faith without sight. We shall have altered our attitude toward it because of God's unfailing help. The darkness and the difficulties, the length of the way and the sense of human loneliness, the very hopelessness and helplessness which we experience will have transfigured by divine alchemy the base elements of self-confidence and self-assertiveness into the gold of God's goodness and grace. When we are changed, life's pathway itself becomes a matter of indifference, except that it continues to lead to the City of the Great King.

You are groping in the darkness with no knowledge as to where to go or what to do? *But God* knows, so go onward in that confidence, because He guides through somber shadows into the golden glow of the sunrising.

GRACE SUFFICIENT

My grace is sufficient for thee — II Corinthians 12:9

So many burdened lives along the way!
  My load seems lighter than the most I see,
And oft I wonder if I could be brave,
  Patient and sweet if they were laid on me.

But God has never said that He would give
  Another's grace without another's thorn;
What matter, since for every day of mine
  Sufficient grace for me comes with the morn?

And though the future brings some heavier cross
  I need not cloud the present with my fears;
I know the grace that is enough today
  Will be sufficient still through all the years.
                    — ANNIE JOHNSON FLINT

7.

BUT GOD IS MY SHIELD

Lord, how are they increased that trouble me! many are they that rise up against me. Many there be which say of my soul, There is no help for him in God. BUT THOU, O LORD, *art a shield for me; my glory, and the lifter up of mine head (Psalm 3:1-3).*

Someone has observed that the New Testament is especially helpful for morning devotions and that the Psalms constitute a comforting pillow for one's head at night. The third Psalm contains something of that thought. In this psalm, David is not ignorant of the stupendous difficulties that surround him. Objectively he observed: "Lord, how are they increased that trouble me! many are they that rise up against me. Many there be which say of my soul, There is no help for him in God."

There is a basic difference in the reaction of a dog and a cat to sudden alarm. When a dog is startled by a loud noise behind him, he is inclined to flee at break-neck speed without trying to ascertain the cause of the fear. Contrariwise, a cat when thus startled will stop, turn around, survey carefully the situation, and then leave or stay as the situation warrants.

We are too much given to running away, or worrying ourselves sick over adversities and calamities. We are to be realistic as to our situation, but we are to remember that God is above and beyond any circumstance. In dismay and difficulty we are to keep looking unto our Lord, with the result that we can run with patience the race of each day.

Like the psalmist we are to declare, "But thou, O Lord, art a shield for me; my glory, and the lifter up of mine head." Then, as did the psalmist, we should make our petition to God and, with the assurance that He has heard, echo his testimony: "I laid me down and slept; I awaked; for the Lord sustained me." After such committal to the Lord and the restful slumber which followed, David was refreshed in spirit and strengthened in body so that he could say, "I will not be afraid of ten thousands of people, that have set themselves against me round about." Believing prayer and physical rest make one fearless in the Lord.

This is the divine antidote for fearfulness. God and one believer make a majority in any problem or perplexity. God is the lifter up of our head because underneath are always the everlasting arms. He gives grace to the humble, but resists the proud. His Name is the strong tower into which we can run and be safe (Proverbs 18:10).

Look the situation over . . . be aware of the dangers . . . then say, *But thou, O Lord, art a shield for me!*

SHUT IN

Shut in — shut in from the ceaseless din
Of the restless world, and its want and sin.
Shut in from its turmoil, care and strife
And all the wearisome round of life.

Shut in, with tears that are spent in vain.
With the dull companionship of pain;
Shut in with the changeless days and hours,
And the bitter knowledge of failing powers.

Shut in with a trio of angels sweet —
Patience and Grace all pain to meet,
With Faith that can suffer and stand and wait,
And lean on the promises strong and great!

Shut in with Christ! Oh, wonderful thought!
Shut in with the peace His sufferings brought;
Shut in with the love that wields the rod —
Oh, company blest! shut in with God!
                              — ANNIE JOHNSON FLINT

8.

BUT GOD IS MERCIFUL

Mine enemies speak evil of me, When shall he die, and his name perish? And if he come to see me, he speaketh vanity: his heart gathereth iniquity to itself; when he goeth abroad, he telleth it. . . . BUT THOU, O LORD, *be merciful unto me, and raise me up, that I may requite them. By this I know that thou favourest me, because mine enemy doth not triumph over me (Psalm 41:5, 6, 10, 11).*

In times of physical weakness caused by disease or exhaustion, all our difficulties and disappointments are magnified beyond their true significance. Weariness and painfulness can distort our perspective so that what really is a matter of small consideration can loom large and threatening to us. It is true that our critics can be cruel and without conscience, and our enemies speak evil against us. Our adversaries appear to be delighted with our adversity and even hope against our recovery. Our foes can be fierce and, what is even worse, our friends can be unfaithful, even false. The experience of the psalmist is quite universal as he declared: "All that hate me whisper together against me: against me do they devise my hurt. An evil disease, say they, cleaveth fast unto him: and now that he lieth he shall rise up no more. Yea, mine own familiar friend, in whom I trusted, which did eat of my bread, hath lifted up his heel against me" (Psalm 41:7-9).

The heart can be utterly discouraged and disconsolate if we pay attention only to people. While not unmindful of our circumstances, we are not to be occupied wholly with

the horizontal; rather, we should have the upward, vertical look toward the Faithful One. Like the psalmist, we are to call upon Him, and even include confession of our sin in that call as the psalmist did, saying, "Lord, be merciful unto me: heal my soul; for I have sinned against thee." One remembers the instruction in James 5:16: "Confess your faults one to another, and pray one for another, that ye may be healed. The effectual fervent prayer of a righteous man availeth much."

In that upward look of faith we also can pray the petition which overrules all that men may do or say. They may be strong and self-confident, ambitious and active in their opposition. Our response is: "But thou, O Lord, be merciful unto me, and raise me up. . . ." That prayer will be answered because of God's mercy and not because of any merit on our part. To the trusting heart comes the same assurance that the psalmist knew after his plea for mercy: "By this I know that thou favourest me, because my enemy doth not triumph over me."

They are many, but the Lord is merciful!
They are mighty, but the Lord is merciful!
His mercy endures forever!

My Prayer

I do not ask that I may steer
    My bark by peaceful shores alone,
Nor that I linger, harbor-bound,
    And sail no stormy seas unknown;
I only ask this boon of Thee:
Be ever in the ship with me.

I do not ask that I may dwell
    From din of battle far removed,
Nor ever feel temptation's force,
    Nor ever know mine armor proved;
I only ask, through Life's long fight,
Grant me the power of Thy might.

I do not ask that I may walk
    Only on smoothly trodden grass,
Nor ever climb the mountain's height
    And trembling, through its dangers pass;
I only ask, on rocks or sand,
The sure upholding of Thy hand.

I dare not pray for any gift
    Upon my pilgrim path to Heaven;
I only ask one thing of Thee:
    Give Thou Thyself and all is given.
I am not strong nor brave nor wise;
Be Thou with me — it shall suffice.

               — Annie Johnson Flint

9.

BUT GOD IS THE JUDGE

I said unto the fools, Deal not foolishly: and to the wicked, Lift not up the horn: lift not up your horn on high: speak not with a stiff neck. For promotion cometh neither from the east, nor from the west, nor from the south. BUT GOD is the judge; he putteth down one, and setteth up another (Psalm 75:4-7).

"Mussolini, who was he?" inquired a young college sophomore less than fifteen years after the close of World War II.

"Hitler, who was he?" inquired another.

It would seem to us who are a bit older and who lived through the days when Fascism in Italy and Nazism in Germany occupied the center of the international stage that anyone would be familiar with these. We heard the boasting and bravado of these two autocrats, and for a time it seemed that their march of triumph would continue indefinitely. Both, however, came to a most ignominious death: Mussolini hanged by his fellow Italians and Hitler a suicide by his own hand.

The psalmist made the inquiry: "Why do the heathen [the nations] rage, and the people imagine a vain thing?" It is because "the kings of the earth set themselves, and the rulers take counsel together, against the Lord, and against his anointed" (Psalm 2:1, 2). They do not take into account the sovereignty of the Most High as declared in Psalm 103:19 — "The Lord hath prepared his throne in the heavens; and his kingdom ruleth over all." God's kingdom is

45

over all earthly government. God always has the last word, even though He may appear to be silent and absent when the wicked are in authority.

Not infrequently God's people have raised the question stated in Psalm 10:1-4: "Why standest thou afar off, O Lord? why hidest thou thyself in times of trouble? The wicked in his pride doth persecute the poor: let them be taken in the devices that they have imagined. For the wicked boasteth of his heart's desire, and blesseth the covetous, whom the Lord abhorreth. The wicked, through the pride of his countenance, will not seek after God: God is not in all his thoughts." Therefore we pray: "Arise, O Lord; O God, lift up thine hand: forget not the humble. Wherefore doth the wicked contemn God? he hath said in his heart, Thou wilt not require it. Thou hast seen it; for thou beholdest mischief and spite, to requite it with thy hand: the poor committeth himself unto thee; thou art the helper of the fatherless" (vss. 12-14).

But God is greater than the greed of the godless and more mighty than their most evil machinations. However high man may exalt himself, God is higher. The Judge of all the earth is above the unjust judgment made by corrupt men, and overrules their cunning and cruelty. The Almighty is patient and painstaking, and desires that sinners come to repentance. However, His longsuffering is not without limit. When God says, "Enough!" the end of some tyrant has come.

We are to have the confidence expressed in Psalm 37:34-36: "Wait on the Lord, and keep his way, and he shall exalt thee to inherit the land: when the wicked are cut off, thou shalt see it. I have seen the wicked in great power, and spreading himself like a green bay tree. Yet

47

he passed away, and, lo, he was not: yea, I sought him, but he could not be found." Puny men may believe themselves to be powerful and permanent, "but God is the judge: he putteth down one, and setteth up another. For in the hand of the Lord there is a cup, and the wine is red; it is full of mixture; and he poureth out of the same: but the dregs thereof, all the wicked of the earth shall wring them out, and drink them" (Psalm 75:7, 8).

BUT WE SEE JESUS

I don't look back, God knows the fruitless efforts,
　　The wasted hours, the sinning, the regrets,
I leave them all with Him who blots the record,
　　And mercifully forgives, and then forgets.

I don't look forward, God sees all the future,
　　The road that, short or long, will lead me home,
And He will face with me its every trial,
　　And bear for me the burdens that may come.

But I look up — into the face of Jesus,
　　For there my heart can rest, my fears are stilled,
And there is joy, and love, and light for darkness,
　　And perfect peace, and every hope fulfilled.

— ANNIE JOHNSON FLINT

10.

BUT GOD IS MY DEFENCE

Who will rise up for me against the evildoers? or who will stand up for me against the workers of iniquity? Unless the Lord had been my help, my soul had almost dwelt in silence. When I said, My foot slippeth; thy mercy, O Lord, held me up. . . . They gather themselves together against the soul of the righteous, and condemn the innocent blood. BUT THE LORD *is my defence; and my God is the rock of my refuge. And he shall bring upon them their own iniquity, and shall cut them off in their own wickedness; yea, the Lord our God shall cut them off (Psalm 94:16-18, 21-23).*

Mankind is intrinsically myopic in matters spiritual. By nature we are creatures of earth who live by sight and not by faith, by feeling and not by the facts of God's revelation. Most of mankind live as though there were no God, utterly oblivious of the truth that the Almighty is aware of every detail of every human life.

"Thou God seest me" is a solemn and searching truth. The psalmist who had come to know the Lord asked equally searching questions, saying: "He that planted the ear, shall he not hear? he that formed the eye, shall he not see? He that chastiseth the heathen [that is, the nations of earth], shall not he correct? he that teacheth man knowledge, shall not he know?" (Psalm 94:9, 10).

The judgment of God, however, seems to linger long and we, like the psalmist, are inclined to inquire: "Lord, how long shall the wicked, how long shall the wicked triumph? How long shall they utter and speak hard things? and all the workers of iniquity boast themselves?" (vss. 3, 4).

The same bewilderment was experienced by the prophet Habakkuk, a contemporary of Jeremiah in the declining days of the kingdom of Judah preceding the long captivity in Babylon. God's servant saw the rise of that empire from the East with its cruelty, brutality, and bloodshed. In perplexity he prayed: "O Lord, thou hast ordained them for judgment; and, O mighty God, thou hast established them for correction. Thou art of purer eyes than to behold evil, and canst not look on iniquity: wherefore lookest thou upon them that deal treacherously, and holdest thy tongue when the wicked devoureth the man that is more righteous than he? And maketh men as the fishes of the sea, as the creeping things, that have no ruler over them?" (1:12-14).

The true heart attitude of the bewildered and bruised was stated in Habakkuk's response: "I will stand upon my watch, and set me upon the tower, and will watch to see what he will say unto me, and what I shall answer when I am reproved" (2:1). To that faith and faithfulness the Most High replied: "Write the vision, and make it plain upon tables, that he may run that readeth it. For the vision is yet for an appointed time, but at the end it shall speak, and not lie: though it tarry, wait for it; because it will surely come, it will not tarry" (2:2, 3). God's righteous judgment seems to tarry; but the trusting heart can wait for it.

In his poem *Fears and Scruples,* Robert Browning gave eloquent expression to the perplexity of a believer who has no immediate answer to the worldly-wise and the wicked:

I can simply wish I might refute you,
Wish my friend would — by a word, a wink —
Bid me stop that foolish mouth, — you brute you!
He keeps absent, — why I cannot think.

51

Never mind! Though foolishness may flout me,
One thing's sure enough; 'Tis neither frost,
No nor fire shall freeze or burn out of me
Thanks for the truth — through falsehood, gained — though lost.

The psalmist came to the same conclusion. He observed
the unconcern of the ungodly toward the Almighty and
their cruelty and craftiness against God's people; yet he
could say, "*But the Lord* is my defence; and my God is the
rock of my refuge. And he shall bring upon them their own
iniquity, and shall cut them off in their own wickedness; yea,
the Lord our God shall cut them off" (Psalm 94:22, 23).

He Giveth More

He giveth more grace — James 4:6.

He increaseth strength — Isaiah 40:29.

Mercy unto you, and peace, and love, be multiplied
— Jude 2.

He giveth more grace when the burdens grow greater,
    He sendeth more strength when the labors increase;
To added affliction He addeth His mercy,
    To multiplied trials, His multiplied peace.

When we have exhausted our store of endurance,
    When our strength has failed ere the day is half done,
When we reach the end of our hoarded resources,
    Our Father's full giving is only begun.

His love has no limit, His grace has no measure,
    His power no boundary known unto men;
For out of His infinite riches in Jesus
    He giveth and giveth and giveth again.

— Annie Johnson Flint

11.

BUT GOD'S MERCY IS EVERLASTING

Like as a father pitieth his children, so the Lord pitieth them that fear him. For he knoweth our frame; he remembereth that we are dust. As for man, his days are as grass: as a flower of the field, so he flourisheth. For the wind passeth over it, and it is gone; and the place thereof shall know it no more. BUT THE MERCY OF THE LORD *is from everlasting to everlasting upon them that fear him, and his righteousness unto children's children; to such as keep his covenant, and to those that remember his commandments to do them (Psalm 103:13-18).*

Our life expectancy may be long because of abounding health, or it may be brief because of lingering and debilitating illness. However long or short human life may be, it is fleeting and uncertain. The psalmist soliloquizes thoughtfully on the brevity of our existence, saying, "As for man, his days are as grass: as a flower of the field, so he flourisheth. For the wind passeth over it, and it is gone; and the place thereof shall know it no more" (Psalm 103:15, 16). In another place the Scripture observes: "The days of our years are threescore years and ten; and if by any reason of strength they be fourscore years, yet is their strength labour and sorrow; for it is soon cut off, and we fly away" (Psalm 90:10).

But the mercy of the Lord — God's compassion and concern for the children of men, His covenant love in our behalf — is not something that passes quickly away. It is, rather, from all eternity past to all eternity future. The God who measures His forgiveness by infinity measures His mercy by eternity. In this same psalm, the Bible declares that God "hath not dealt with us after our sins; nor rewarded us according to our iniquities. For as the heaven is high above the earth, so great is his mercy toward them that fear him. As far as the east is from the west, so far hath he removed our transgressions from us" (Psalm 103:10-12). Fathomless is His forgiveness and measureless is His mercy; upon such strength our hearts should be established.

Not only is His mercy unfailing to those who fear Him (that is, who love God, trust Him, worship Him), but His righteousness is "unto children's children." Our part is to walk uprightly in obedience to the light of God's Word and will (that is, "remember his commandments to do them") and then trust that our children and grandchildren likewise receive the Savior as their own and thereby know the illimitable mercy of the Most High.

We are finite, but God is infinite.

Our days are few or many, but He is eternal.

Our faithfulness to Him is measured by the brief span of our life, but His mercy to our children and children's children is from everlasting to everlasting.

COUNT IT DONE

A father wrote to his son,
  Who was faraway from home;
"I have sent you a beautiful gift,
  It may be delayed, but 'twill come;
It is what you have wanted most,
  And have asked for many days;"
And before the child received the gift
  He voiced his thanks and praise.

Our Father saith unto us:
  "Your need shall be supplied;
Ask and receive that your joy be filled,
  And My joy in you abide."
Shall we wait to thank till we see
  The answer to every prayer?
Forbear to praise till we feel
  The lifted pressure of care?
Nay, let us trust His word
  And know that the thing is done,
For His promise is just as sure
  As a father's to his son.

— ANNIE JOHNSON FLINT

56

12

BUT GOD IS IN THE HEAVENS

Not unto us, O Lord, not unto us, but unto thy name give glory, for thy mercy, and for thy truth's sake. Wherefore should the heathen say, Where is now their God? BUT *our* GOD *is in the heavens: he hath done whatsoever he hath pleased (Psalm 115:1-3).*

The prophet Micah asked his people a searching question. Judgment was impending, and the contemporaries of the prophet seemed to pay little heed to the dangers they were facing. Therefore he called to them (Micah 2:7): "O thou that art named the house of Jacob, is the spirit of the Lord straitened? are these his doings? do not my words do good to him that walketh uprightly?"

The Spirit of God is not straitened (restricted, limited) except by our unbelief and disobedience. Psalm 78:41 speaks of the Israelites in their desert journey to the Promised Land and declares that "they turned back and tempted God, and limited the Holy One of Israel." When the Lord Jesus came into "his own country" (that is, the area of Nazareth and Capernaum in Galilee), He said, "A prophet is not without honour, but in his own country, and among his own kin, and in his own house." The gospel account records further: "And he could there do no mighty work, save that he laid his hands upon a few sick folk, and healed them. And he marvelled because of their unbelief. And he went round about the villages, teaching" (Mark 6:4-6).

The warning against unbelief is written large in the Scriptures. Jeremiah had to face the question that we also cannot avoid: "Behold, I am the Lord, the God of all flesh: is there anything too hard for me?" (Jeremiah 32:27). To that same prophet was given the promise recorded in chapter 29, verse 11, which in the Rotherham translation reads: "For I know the plan that I am planning for you, saith the Lord, plans of welfare and not of calamity, to give you a future and a hope." God's thoughts, indeed, are "peace, and not evil" for His trusting children. Has He not told us in Psalm 84:11, 12: "For the Lord God is a sun and shield: the Lord will give grace and glory: no good thing will he withhold from them that walk uprightly. O Lord of hosts, blessed is the man that trusteth in thee."

Our part is to be utterly obedient to all the will of God as best we know it, and to believe what the Most High has told us in His Word. Even then it may be for us, as in the experience of the psalmist, that there are those who say, "Where is now their God?" Our response is like his:

"But our God is in the heavens: he hath done whatsoever he hath pleased." And we know that His plans are for our temporal and eternal welfare, and not for calamity (Jeremiah 29:11, Rotherham).

I Have Set the Lord

I have set the Lord always before me — Psalm 16:8.

I set Thy love between the world and me,
O Lord, its cruelty, its wrong, its scorn;
They cannot reach me through Thy tenderness
That once for me their worst has known and borne.

I set Thy cross between my sins and me,
That so their shadow darken not my days,
Nor rob my nights of rest. Thy blood blots out
The long indictment from my shrinking gaze.

I set Thy prayers between my doubts and me,
That so my faith shall fail not, but abide,
Though tried and tested sore; that shield shall serve
All fiery darts to quench or turn aside.

I set Thy strength between my foes and me,
And walk, so guarded, panoplied and girt,
Through dangers seen and unseen, unafràid;
Through flames unscorched and raging waves unhurt.

I set Thy thoughts between my thoughts and me,
The calm, pure visions of Thy holy mind,
Till nothing that disturbs me or defiles,
Into my heart or soul can entrance find.

I set Thy self between my self and me,
And losing mine, Thy life abundant gain;
Take Thy sufficiency for my deep need,
And to Thy perfect stature so attain.

— ANNIE JOHNSON FLINT

13.

BUT GOD HELPED ME

It is better to trust in the Lord than to put confidence in man. It is better to trust in the Lord than to put confidence in princes. All nations compassed me about: but in the name of the Lord will I destroy them. They compassed me about; yea, they compassed me about: but in the name of the Lord I will destroy them. They compassed me about like bees; they are quenched as the fire of thorns: for in the name of the Lord I will destroy them. Thou hast thrust sore at me that I might fall: BUT THE LORD *helped me. The Lord is my strength and song, and is become my salvation (Psalm 118:8-14).*

"Be strong in the Lord, and in the power of his might. Put on the whole armour of God, that ye may be able to stand against the wiles of the devil" is the exhortation in Ephesians 6:10, 11. The Christian has a fierce and determined foe. Spiritual warfare is not a figment of imagination nor a mere figure of speech. The instruction in Ephesians continues: "For we wrestle not against flesh and blood, but against principalities, against powers, against the rulers of the darkness of this world, against spiritual wickedness in high places" (v. 12).

Bunyan, in *Pilgrim's Progress,* gives a graphic account of Christian's encounter with Apollyon. After the delightful visit in the Palace Beautiful where he received encouragement, instruction, and especially armor for his warfare, Christian descended into the Valley of Humiliation. Then it was that the enemy appeared. The pilgrim wondered whether he should go back or stand his ground. Then relates Bunyan: "But he considered, again, that he had no armour for his back, and therefore thought that to turn the back to him might give him greater advantage with ease to pierce him with his darts; therefore he resolved to venture and stand his ground; 'for,' thought he, 'had I no more in mine eye than the saving of my life, it would be the best way to stand.'"

The encounter was dreadful. After attacking Christian's testimony and faith, the enemy threw a flaming dart; "but Christian had a shield in his hand, with which he caught it, and so prevented the danger of that." Finally, Satan caused Christian to drop his sword. The sword of the Spirit "is the word of God," without which we cannot prevail against our wicked opponent. Christian was able to retrieve his sword, saying, "Rejoice not against me, O my enemy: when I fall, I shall arise," which he quoted from Micah 7:8. With his sword he defeated the foe, who then fled.

Like Bunyan's pilgrim, we are to learn to resist the devil and he will flee from us (James 5:7) and thus we learn that "in all these things we are more than conquerors through him that loved us" (Romans 8:37). Then ours is also the testimony of the psalmist:

"Thou has thrust sore at me that I might fall: *but the Lord* helped me. The Lord is my strength and song, and is become my salvation."

"I Shall Yet Praise Him"

Psalm 42:5, 11

I shall yet praise Him — though blossoms have withered,
   Empty the fold is and barren the field,
All the fair promise of harvest has vanished,
   Fig-tree and olive have failed in their yield.

I shall yet praise Him — though now the mists
      shroud me,
Though through the darkness there shineth no star,
Though long delayed be the word of His counsel,
   And to all seeming He hideth afar.

I shall yet praise Him for victory given;
   Though fierce the sifting, His prayer cannot fail;
Till the fourth watch He may leave me in darkness;
   Then clouds shall lift and the light shall prevail.

I shall yet praise Him who knoweth my pathway,
   For all His leading through desert and sea,
For the sure promise that standeth forever,
   For all His purpose fulfilled unto me.

I shall yet praise Him — mute mouth filled with laughter,
   Silent lips opened and tongue tuned to song;
Surely praise waiteth; joy, sown for my reaping,
   Cometh to harvest, though lingering long.

                 — Annie Johnson Flint

14.

BUT GOD HAS RESPECT TO THE LOWLY

In the day when I cried thou answeredst me, and strengthenedst me with strength in my soul. All the kings of the earth shall praise thee, O Lord, when they hear the words of thy mouth. Yea, they shall sing in the ways of the Lord: for great is the glory of the Lord. Though the Lord be high, yet hath he respect unto the lowly: but the proud he knoweth afar off (Psalm 138:3-6).

In the Bible there is much commendation for humility and, conversely, much condemnation for pride and self-sufficiency. "Everyone that is proud in heart is an abomination to the Lord," declares Proverbs 16:5, adding in verse 18, "Pride goeth before destruction, and the haughty spirit before a fall."

"Him that hath an high look and a proud heart will not I suffer," declares the Almighty in Psalm 101:5, who also declares that, "The fear of the Lord is to hate evil: pride, and arrogancy, and the evil way, and the froward mouth, do I hate" (Proverbs 8:13). Pride was the cause for Satan's fall when he was "the anointed cherub" in the presence of God (Ezekiel 28:14).

The Bible, therefore, teaches that a young and inexperienced Christian should not be placed in a position of large responsibility. First Timothy 3:6 states that an elder should be "not a novice, lest being lifted up with pride he fall into the condemnation of the devil."

"Before honor is humility," says Proverbs 15:33, and adds in 29:23, "A man's pride shall bring him low: but honour shall uphold the humble in spirit." The Lord Jesus taught that "whosoever shall exalt himself shall be abased; and he that shall humble himself shall be exalted" (Matthew 23:12). The Most High resists the proud but provides His grace for the lowly of heart (James 4:6). When King Nebuchadnezzar congratulated himself saying, "Is not this great Babylon, that I have built for the house of the kingdom by the might of my power, and for the honor of my majesty?" he was stricken with insanity, and for seven years lived like a beast in the field. When his rationality was returned, he said with all humility: "Now I Nebuchadnezzar praise and extol and honour the King of heaven, all whose works are truth, and his ways judgment: and those that walk in pride he is able to abase" (Daniel 4:30, 37).

"Learn of me," said the Savior, "for I am meek and lowly in heart, and ye shall find rest for your soul." God has compassion and commendation for the contrite in heart, and gives honor to the humble and balm to the broken in heart.

But the proud God knows afar off. God's people need not be disturbed by them, because the Almighty is able to abase them in His own time and way.

"I BELIEVE GOD"

I believe God, that it shall be even as it was told me
— Acts 27:35.

"I believe" — but, do I? Am I sure?
Can I trust my trusting to endure?
Can I hope that my belief will last?
Will my hand forever hold Him fast?
Am I certain I am saved from sin?
Do I feel His presence here within?
Do I hear Him tell me that He cares?
Do I see the answers to my prayers?
Do no fears my confidence assail?
Do I know my faith will never fail?

"I believe" — ay, do I! I believe
He will never fail me, never leave;
I believe He holds me, and I know
His strong hand will never let me go;
Seeing, hearing, feeling — what are these?
Given or withheld as He shall please.
I believe in Him and what He saith;
I have faith in Him, not in my faith
That may fail, tomorrow or today;
Trust may weaken, feeling pass away,
Thoughts grow weary, anxious or depressed;
I believe in God — and here I rest.

— ANNIE JOHNSON FLINT

68

15.

BUT GOD REVEALS THE UNKNOWN

The king answered and said to Daniel, whose name was Belteshazzar, Art thou able to make known unto me the dream which I have seen, and the interpretation thereof? Daniel answered in the presence of the king, and said, The secret which the king hath demanded cannot the wise men, the astrologers, the magicians, the soothsayers, shew unto the king; BUT there is a GOD in heaven that revealeth secrets, and maketh known to the king Nebuchadnezzar what shall be in the latter days (Daniel 2:26-28).

There is delightful, and likewise divine, sarcasm in the observation that the "foolishness of God is wiser than men, and the weakness of God is stronger than men" (I Corinthians 1:25). That same Scripture goes on to declare: "For ye see your calling, brethren, how that not many wise men after the flesh, not many mighty, not many noble, are called: but God hath chosen the foolish things of the world to confound the wise; and God hath chosen the weak things of the world to confound the things which are mighty; and base things of the world, and things which are despised, hath God chosen, yea, and things which are not, to bring to nought things which are: that no flesh should glory in his presence" (vss. 26-29).

Human wisdom and resourcefulness have their limitations, but God has made available resources which are unlimited. For the trusting child of God there is "the peace that passeth understanding" (Philippians 4:7) and there is "the love of Christ which passeth knowledge," as stated in

Ephesians 3:19. The mercy of God is measured by the height of heaven and His forgiveness by the distance of east from west (Psalm 103:11, 12). God's ways are always higher than our ways, as high as heaven is above the earth (Isaiah 55:9). And who can determine that infinite distance?

Nebuchadnezzar called the wisest men in his Chaldean kingdom to declare to him his dream and to explain it, but none could do so. Daniel knew that in himself there was no such insight or understanding. He was sure, however, that "there is a God in heaven that revealeth secrets." "Revelation" means the making known by God to us that which we could not possibly learn by search and research. What we cannot find out for ourselves, He can make clear to the prayerful and obedient.

God places no premium on ignorance; rather, He has revealed Himself in the Bible, which is His special revelation, and in creation, the universe, which is His general revelation. From these we are to learn His ways and His works, His salvation and His sustaining power. Reverence and humility are essential to any true understanding of God's revelation. Pride and presumption will pervert the evidence God gives to men.

Sidney Lanier observed:

"Vainly the mind of man might resolve it;

Plainly the mind of a child could solve it."

That is the poet's way of asserting what our Lord said: "I thank thee, O Father, Lord of heaven and earth, because thou hast hid these things from the wise and prudent, and hast revealed them unto babes. Even so, Father: for so it seemed good in thy sight" (Matthew 11:25, 26).

We may not know, but God knows. Our part is to be teachable and true to all we are taught.

71

Do Thou for Me

Do Thou for me, God — my God,
Helpless, I appeal to Thee;
What is best I cannot tell,
What is right I cannot see.
Blind, I dread to stand or go,
And I fear to lose the way,
For I know not what to do
And I know not how to pray.
Hear my cry: "Do Thou for me —
I can trust it all with Thee."

Fight Thou for me, God — my God;
How shall I my foes withstand?
I should only fail and yield;
Take the battle in Thy hand.
Thou my Rock, my Strength, my Shield,
Lo, I flee to Thee for aid;
Weak — so weak — but be my strength
Perfect through that weakness made.
Hear my cry: "Fight Thou for me —
More than conqueror I shall be."

Live Thou for me, God — my God
Come Thou and abide in me,
That my sinful self may die,
Daily crucified with Thee.
Think my thoughts and speak my words,
Move my lips, my hands, my feet,
Till Thou art unveiled in me
And Thine image is complete.
Hear my cry: "Live Thou for me —
Thus alone I live for Thee."

— ANNIE JOHNSON FLINT

16.

BUT WITH GOD ALL IS POSSIBLE

Then said Jesus unto his disciples, Verily I say unto you, That a rich man shall hardly enter into the kingdom of heaven. And again I say unto you, It is easier for a camel to go through the eye of a needle, than for a rich man to enter into the kingdom of God. When his disciples heard it, they were exceedingly amazed, saying, Who then can be saved? But Jesus beheld them, and said unto them, With men this is impossible; BUT WITH GOD *all things are possible (Matthew 19:23-26).*

God's Word presents paradoxes that are perplexing to the unbeliever or to that one untaught in the truth of divine revelation. From a human point of view, two factors may appear to be mutually exclusive, but not so with God. In Hebrews 11:27 we read that "Moses endured as seeing him who is invisible." See the invisible? Impossible, we say. Scripture, however, declares: "Our light affliction, which is but for a moment, worketh for us a far more exceeding and eternal weight of glory; while we look not at the things which are seen, but at the things which are not seen: for the things which are seen are temporal; but the things which are not seen are eternal" (II Corinthians 4:17, 18).

The invisible is discerned by faith, as we read in the 11th chapter of Hebrews, *The Amplified New Testament,* vss. 1, 3, 6:

> Now faith is the assurance (the confirmation, the title-deed) of the things [we] hope for, being the proof of things [we] do not see and the conviction of their reality — faith perceiving as real fact what is not revealed

to the senses. . . . By faith we understand that the worlds [during the successive ages] were framed — fashioned, put in order and equipped for their intended purpose — by the word of God, so that what we see was not made out of things which are visible. . . . But without faith it is impossible to please and be satisfactory to Him. For whoever would come near to God must (necessarily) believe that God exists and that He is the Rewarder of those who earnestly and diligently seek Him (out).

Likewise the Bible speaks of doing the impossible. The patriarch, Abraham, was a man of faith of whom it is stated that he believed God "who quickeneth the dead and calleth those things which be not as though they were. Who against hope believed in hope, that he might become the father of many nations, according to that which was spoken, So shall thy seed be. . . . He staggered not at the promise of God through unbelief; but was strong in faith, giving glory to God; and being fully persuaded that, what he had promised, he was able also to perform" (Romans 4:17-21).

When the disciples saw the rich young ruler go sadly away, after which the Lord Jesus made the observation, "It is easier for a camel to go through the eye of a needle, than for a rich man to enter the kingdom of God," they inquired with amazement: "Who then can be saved?"

No one can be saved by trusting in himself, in his merits or character, in his benevolence toward others because of his money. The Bible says plainly: "You must know (recognize) that you were redeemed (ransomed) from the useless (fruitless) way of living inherited by tradition from [your] forefathers, not with corruptible things [such as] silver and gold, but [you were purchased] with the precious blood of Christ, the Messiah, like that of a [sacrificial] lamb without blemish or spot" (*Amplified New Testament*, I Peter 1:18, 19).

Of course rich people, or anyone, can be saved if in all humility and penitence they receive the Savior. In themselves this is an impossibility, *but with God* all things are possible!

THE UNBOUGHT GOOD

What would our land be worth to us,
    The land we sell and buy,
And fence about, and call our own,
    Without God's open sky
To hold the sunset's rose and gold,
    The white clouds floating high?

What would our fields bring forth for us
    Without the gifts He sends,
Without the sunshine and the rain
    On which our bread depends,
His little water-brooks to flow,
    His birds to be our friends?

Oh, as the land without the sky
    That ever bends above,
So barren and so desolate
    Our lives without His love;
The blessings that no gold can buy
    Our greatest riches prove.

— ANNIE JOHNSON FLINT

17

BUT GOD SAID TO HIM, THOU FOOL

And he said unto them. Take heed, and beware of covetousness: for a man's life consisteth not in the abundance of the things which he possesseth. And he spake a parable unto them, saying, The ground of a certain rich man brought forth plentifully: and he thought within himself, saying, What shall I do, because I have no room where to bestow my fruits? And he said, This will I do: I will pull down my barns, and build greater; and there will I bestow all my fruits and my goods. And I will say to my soul, Soul, thou hast much goods laid up for many years; take thine ease, eat, drink, and be merry. But God said unto him, Thou fool, this night thy soul shall be required of thee: then whose shall those things be, which thou hast provided? So is he that layeth up treasure for himself, and is not rich toward God" (Luke 12:15-21).

The Bible has much to say on material values as well as on spiritual reality. We are taught to be careful and grateful for all that is provided for us, and not to be wasteful. After the feeding of the five thousand the Lord Jesus had the disciples gather up all the fragments, and twelve large baskets were filled for future use. The disciples were not to be presumptuous nor prodigal just because much had been provided for them. "If riches increase, set not your heart upon them," declares Psalm 62:10. Taught the Savior: "Lay not up for yourselves treasures upon earth, where moth and rust doth corrupt, and where thieves break through and steal: but lay up for yourselves treasures in heaven, where neither moth nor rust doth corrupt, and where thieves do

not break through nor steal: for where your treasure is, there will your heart be also" (Matthew 6:19-21).

The danger to which our Lord referred is covetousness, which is destructive of spiritual life. Therefore we have the exhortation of I Timothy 6:6-10. "But godliness with contentment is great gain. For we brought nothing into this world, and it is certain we can carry nothing out. And having food and raiment let us be therewith content. But they that will be rich fall into temptation and a snare, and into many foolish and hurtful lusts, which drown men in destruction and perdition. For the love of money is the root of all evil; which while some coveted after, they have erred from the faith, and pierced themselves through with many sorrows."

A man of God observed of a fellow Christian, whose business was prospering, that there was the danger of self-centeredness and self-sufficiency. In conversation he inquired, "What makes the difference between a window and a mirror?" In response his friend observed that one receives light through a window, and likewise through it he can see others; while in a mirror one sees only himself. "It is the silver coating on the back of the mirror," observed the faithful man of God, "that turns a window into a mirror."

Declared the Lord Jesus: "Take heed, and beware of covetousness: for a man's life consisteth not in the abundance of the things which he possesseth" (Luke 12:15). To illustrate that truth, He added the parable of the rich fool who was so prosperous that he did not have place for all his crops; and who said, "Soul, thou hast much goods laid up for many years; take thine ease, eat, drink, and be merry" (v. 19).

But God said. . . .

That farmer was no fool in material things; but he was a fool because he never took God, nor his own soul, nor eternity, into consideration. What does it profit us if we should gain the world, yet lose our own soul?

PASSING THROUGH

When thou passest through the waters, they shall not overflow thee — Isaiah 43:2

"When Thou passest through the waters,"
  Deep the waves may be, and cold,
But Jehovah is our refuge
  And His promise is our hold;
For the Lord Himself hath said it,
  He the faithful God and true;
"When thou comest to the waters,
  Thou shalt *not go down,* but *through.*

Seas of sorrow, seas of trial,
  Bitterest anguish, fiercest pain,
Rolling surges of temptation,
  Sweeping over heart and brain,
They shall never overflow us,
  For we know His word is true;
All His waves and all His billows
  He will *lead us safely through.*

Threatening breakers of destruction,
  Doubt's insidious undertow,
Shall not sink us, shall not drag us
  Out to ocean depths of woe;
For His promise shall sustain us,
  Praise the Lord, whose word is true!
We shall not go down or under,
  He hath said, "Thou passest *through.*"

         — ANNIE JOHNSON FLINT

18.

BUT I HAVE PRAYED FOR THEE

*And the Lord said, Simon, Simon, behold, Satan hath
desired to have you, that he may sift you as wheat:* BUT I
*have prayed for thee, that thy faith fail not: and when thou
art converted, strengthen thy brethren. And he said unto
him, Lord, I am ready to go with thee, both into prison,
and to death. And he said, I tell thee, Peter, the cock shall
not crow this day, before that thou shalt thrice deny that
thou knowest me (Luke 22:31-34).*

Peter was perfectly sincere when he asserted, "Lord, I
am ready to go with thee, both into prison, and to death."
He meant every word! He was completely devoted to his
Lord and fully determined to go with Him anywhere, even
at the cost of his own life. With the bold courage of a fish-
erman who had sailed through storms on the Sea of Galilee, he was unafraid of any foe; but he was unfamiliar with
the instability of his own heart. The Savior appreciated the
fervor and promised faithfulness of Peter, but he had a true
estimate of Peter's steadfastness.

In His faithfulness to Peter and the others, the Lord
Jesus warned them of what soon was to transpire in Geth-
semane's garden. He Himself was entering into dreadful
conflict with the prince of this world, even Satan. He knew
that the great enemy of God and of mankind would do all
in his power to destroy both the Savior and His disciples.
Therefore, the Lord spoke very tenderly to Peter, calling
him by his first name and saying, "Simon, Simon, behold,
Satan hath desired to have you, that he may sift you as
wheat." The figure of speech is taken from the threshing

81

floor, familiar still to the inhabitants of Palestine. The chaff is separated from the wheat by the flail. The Lord Jesus was telling Peter that soon he would undergo dreadful temptation and punishment from the prince of darkness, just as though he were a stalk of wheat under the flail.

"But I have prayed for thee, that thy faith fail not," said the Savior to Simon Peter. He wanted His follower to have the assurance in the time of deepest darkness and despair that he was the object of his Lord's prayer. Peter had often heard the Lord pray and had seen the answers to prayer. He had been with his Lord at the grave of Lazarus and had heard the Lord Jesus say, "Father, I thank thee that thou hast heard me; and I know that thou hearest me always" (John 11:41, 42). Peter did fail; but in answer to prayer he was restored and became a channel of strength for his fellow believers.

We, like Peter, undergo times of deep testing. While we are fearful and frustrated therein, we should remember that the Lord Jesus is now our Great High Priest in heaven. He ever lives to intercede on our behalf (Romans 8:34; I John 2:1, 2). The Scripture declares plainly: "Seeing then that we have a great high priest, that is passed into the heavens, Jesus the Son of God, let us hold fast our profession. For we have not an high priest which cannot be touched with the feeling of our infirmities; but was in all points tempted like as we are, yet without sin. Let us therefore come boldly unto the throne of grace, that we may obtain mercy, and find grace to help in time of need" (Hebrews 4:14-16).

We are tested, but not forsaken; bruised and bewildered, but not abandoned; utterly cast down, but not destroyed, because of Him who says to us today as He did to Peter long ago: *"But I have prayed for thee, that thy faith fail not"*!

No chastening for the present seemeth joyous, but grievous;
nevertheless afterward it yieldeth the peaceable fruit of
righteousness — Hebrews 12:11.

I was so happy in my lot,
    I was so glad of work or play,
I only asked that I might walk
    With others on life's common way;
My Father let the sorrow come
    That blotted out the sunlit skies,
That stopped the toil of busy hands
    And turned my laughter into sighs.

I was so sorrowful, so spent,
    I only asked to dwell apart,
And in the silence and the dark
    To nurse my bruised and broken heart;
My Father came and took my hand
    And led me forth in paths unknown,
He filled my days with crowding cares,
    He would not let me weep alone.

But, looking backward now, I know
    How wise and kind He was to me,
The clouds all gone, the shadows fled,
    His glorious afterward I see;
If He had left me to myself
    I know the joys I should have lost,
The good that I have lacked or missed,
    How much I gained, how small the cost.

And shall I doubt His love today
    Because once more the mists arise,
Because His hand, though leading still,
    Is hidden from my blinded eyes?
Nay, help me to remember, Lord.
    As 'neath the chastening rod I bow,
Thy wondrous dealing past, and trust
    Thine afterward for this dark now.
            — ANNIE JOHNSON FLINT

19

BUT GOD THE HOLY SPIRIT

*These things have I spoken unto you, being yet present
with you.* BUT THE COMFORTER, *which is the Holy Ghost,
whom the Father will send in my name, he shall teach you
all things, and bring all things to your remembrance, whatsoever I have said unto you. Peace I leave with you, my
peace I give unto you: not as the world giveth, give I unto
you. Let not your heart be troubled, neither let it be afraid
(John 14:25-27).*

The Lord Jesus Christ is the Teacher of teachers! The
centuries of human history have known many eminent in-
structors: Aristotle, Plato, Socrates, Augustine, Calvin, to
mention but a few; and one should include Confucius and
Marcus Aurelius; but Jesus of Nazareth is superior to all of
them. With winsome and yet searching simplicity He taught
the most profound truths about Deity and humanity, about
the Creator and the creation, and yet His illustrations came
from commonplace things like the birds of the air and the
flowers of the field.

We wish we had lived in the day of the Lord Jesus so
that we could have known Him for ourselves, could have
seen His miracles of compassion and healing, could have
heard His teaching. Had we been among the multitude who
heard His Sermon on the Mount, we would have agreed
with the rest that He taught with authority and not with
the pedantic plodding of the scribes. We would have mar-
veled at His deep insight into the law of God as given to
Moses, His illumination of the teaching of the prophets, as

Isaiah and Daniel, and the psalmists, like David and Asaph. We would have understood well what the soldiers meant in their report when they said that "never man spake like this man"! Of course the common people heard the Savior gladly!

But we did not live then. Furthermore, the Lord Jesus is not here on earth anywhere so that we can go to Him for His instruction and counsel. However, another Teacher, the equal of the Savior, is here in the world. He is the Holy Spirit who dwells in our hearts by faith. Of Him the Lord Jesus said: "I will pray the Father, and he shall give you another Comforter, that he may abide with you for ever; even the Spirit of truth; whom the world cannot receive, because it seeth him not, neither knoweth him: but ye know him; for he dwelleth with you, and shall be in you" (John 14:16, 17).

All that the Lord Jesus was to His disciples in their day, the Holy Spirit can be to us today. The term "Comforter," is translated in the *Amplified New Testament*: "Counsellor, Helper, Intercessor, Advocate, Strengthener, and Stand-by." The Holy Spirit is *another* Comforter — that is, Someone just like the Lord Jesus. It is He who brings divine consolation through the Scriptures to our troubled hearts. He is our Counsellor, to whom we can go for guidance. He is the Spirit of truth and of wisdom. He is our unfailing Helper, the One who is always alongside to grant strength and grace. He is our Intercessor who teaches us to pray according to the will of God. He is our Advocate, the One who pleads our cause, just as the risen Savior now at the right hand of God is our Advocate in heaven. The Paraclete strengthens and establishes our hearts in the faith, and as Stand-by He never leaves nor forsakes us.

The Comforter is also our Teacher. He is *another*

Teacher, one just like the Lord Jesus. Long centuries ago He gave His inspiration to the prophets and apostles so that they wrote down, for their generation and for all time and eternity, the Bible, the Word of the living God. The Bible declares plainly: "All Scripture is given by inspiration of God" (II Timothy 3:16). He who gave the Word in the first place is without doubt the one who best understands the Scriptures and can explain them to God's people. Depend upon Him for His instruction as you carefully read the Bible and compare Scripture with Scripture.

The Teacher of the disciples left them and ascended into heaven; *but* the Comforter, the Third Person of the blessed Trinity, is here to teach us all things pertaining to the truth of God as revealed in the Bible and in the creation.

THE TWO SUFFICIENTS

Sufficient unto the day is the evil thereof — Matthew 6:34.
My grace is sufficient for thee — II Corinthians 12:9.

Evil shall pass with the day that brought it,
    As the sea is stayed by the barrier land;
When the Giver of Good shall say, "No farther,"
    And bid the foeman restrain his hand;
But the grace of the Lord outstays the evil,
    Outlasts the darkness, outruns the morn,
Outwatches the stars in their nightly vigil,
    And the foe that returns with the day re-born,
As he left it unwearied, shall find it unworn.

— ANNIE JOHNSON FLINT

20.

BUT GOD THE LORD SAID, GO THY WAY

*And there was a certain disciple at Damascus, named
Ananias; and to him said the Lord in a vision, Ananias. And
he said, Behold, I am here, Lord. And the Lord said unto
him, Arise, and go into the street which is called Straight,
and enquire in the house of Judas for one called Saul, of
Tarsus: for, behold, he prayeth. And hath seen in a vision
a man named Ananias coming in, and putting his hand on
him, that he might receive his sight. Then Ananias answered, Lord, I have heard by many of this man, how much
evil he hath done to thy saints at Jerusalem: and here he
hath authority from the chief priests to bind all that call
on thy name. BUT THE LORD said unto him, Go thy way:
for he is a chosen vessel unto me, to bear my name before
the Gentiles, and kings, and the children of Israel: for I
will shew him how great things he must suffer for my name's
sake (Acts 9:10-16).*

Not infrequently God's assignments to us are quite contrary to human reasoning or choice. We, like Ananias of
Damascus, have every reason to question the leading of the
Lord. In his case, he was given instructions to go to the very
person who had come to the city with authority to exter-
minate the Christians. Ananias had every reason to fear Saul
of Tarsus and no reason to trust him.

Ananias, however, did not know that Saul had met the
Lord Jesus on the road to the city, that the persecutor had
become a penitent fellow believer. Without doubt the Christians in Damascus had prayed for protection, for safety and

deliverance from this cruel and fanatical religionist. I wonder if they ever prayed for his conversion to Christ? At any rate, God had done "exceeding abundantly above all" that the Christians were able to think. Paul had become a fellow Christian, a humble servant of the Lord Jesus, and he needed the Lord's help through some fellow believer.

We are prone to argue with the Lord against an assignment that seems to us to be difficult, dangerous, and impossible. We proclaim to Him the peril and express fears that seem wholly justifiable to us. But God knows why He guides us into strange ways, into apparent dangers. Our part is to trust Him fully, to obey Him implicitly, to follow our instructions faithfully. Who can foretell the outcome of our trusting and obeying?

We say, "Lord, I have heard thus and so . . . ."

But the Lord says, "Go thy way!" It is the way of complete obedience, of faith and faithfulness. The result will prove the rightness of the orders.

He Is Risen

He is risen! Earth awakes
And her prison house forsakes.
Hear the glad bird-voices sing —
"Where, O Death, is now thy sting?"
Winds their silver trumpets blow —
"He hath conquered every foe."
Soft the murmuring waters say —
"Lo, the stone is rolled away."
    He is risen, He is risen,
Christ the Lord is risen to-day.

He is risen! Heart, rejoice,
Hear you not the angel's voice?
Though you wait beside the tomb,
There is light within its gloom:
Grave, where is thy victory?
He hath set thy captives free,
He hath robbed thee of thy prey,
They with Him shall live alway.
    He is risen, He is risen,
Christ the Lord is risen to-day.

— Annie Johnson Flint

21

BUT GOD RAISED HIM FROM THE DEAD

Men and brethren, children of the stock of Abraham, and whosoever among you feareth God, to you is the word of this salvation sent. For they that dwell at Jerusalem, and their rulers, because they knew him not, nor yet the voices of the prophets which are read every sabbath day, they have fulfilled them in condemning him. And though they found no cause of death in him, yet desired they Pilate that he should be slain. And when they had fulfilled all that was written of him, they took him down from the tree, and laid him in a sepulchre. BUT GOD raised him from the dead: and he was seen many days of them which came up with him from Galilee to Jerusalem, who are his witnesses unto the people (Acts 13:26-31).

The long history of mankind shows the rise of religious leaders who drew to themselves a large following and whose teachings now constitute a religion. These men have died. For most of them the place of their burial is known and these places have become shrines to their followers. Christianity has no such culmination to the ministry and message of its Founder. We Christians have an empty sepulcher and a risen Savior. He is not dead, but is alive forevermore!

The resurrection of the Savior is an integral part of the gospel message. It was given large importance in the dynamic preaching of the early Christians. Their message, summarized in I Corinthians 15:3, 4, states: "For I delivered unto you first of all that which I also received, how that Christ died for our sins according to the scriptures; and that

he was buried, and that he rose again the third day according to the scriptures."

In presenting the Gospel for the first time to his fellow countrymen in Asia Minor, the apostle Paul began with Israel's history which showed that God had called them out of Egypt and given them the land of Canaan. After the era of the judges, there began the kingdom. To David, the second king of Israel, God made promise of a Savior. In the fulness of time the Lord Jesus came. As prophesied by Isaiah, the Lord was "despised and rejected of men, a man of sorrows and acquainted with grief." In their resentment against His message and their greed for their own position, the leaders of the people prevailed upon Pilate to have the Lord Jesus crucified.

But God raised Him from the dead!

Because He died for our sins and rose again, we have forgiveness of sin, newness of life even now, and assurance of everlasting life in His presence beyond the grave. Even now by the Scriptures and the indwelling Holy Spirit we are to realize "the exceeding greatness of his power to us-ward who believe, according to the working of his mighty power, which he wrought in Christ, when he raised him from the dead, and set him at his own right hand in the heavenly places, far above all principality, and power, and might, and dominion, and every name that is named, not only in this world, but also in that which is to come . . ." (Ephesians 1:19-21).

All this because God the Father raised the Lord Jesus Christ from the dead!

Death is the common lot of all mankind. God's true prophets of old like Isaiah, Jeremiah, and Daniel have died. The prophets of false religions have all died. Jesus of Nazareth was crucified, and He died; *but God* raised Him from the dead to be the Savior of all them that receive Him.

SOMETIMES

*Quenched the violence of fire, escaped the edge of the
swordj; . . . and others . . . were slain with the sword*
— *Hebrews 11:34, 35, 37.*

Sometimes the lions' mouths are shut;
Sometimes God bids us fight or fly;
Sometimes He feeds us by the brook;
Sometimes the flowing stream runs dry.

Sometimes the burning flames are quenched;
Sometimes with sevenfold heat they glow;
Sometimes His hand divides the waves;
Sometimes His billows overflow.

Sometimes He turns the sword aside;
Sometimes He lets the sharp blade smite;
Sometimes our foes are at our heels,
Sometimes He hides us from their sight.

We may not choose, nor would we dare,
The path in which our feet shall tread;
Enough that He that path hath made,
And He Himself shall walk ahead.

The danger that His love allows
Is safer than our fears may know;
The peril that His care permits
Is our defence where'er we go.

— ANNIE JOHNSON FLINT

22

BUT GOD THE SPIRIT GUIDED THEM

Now when they had gone throughout Phrygia and the region of Galatia, and were forbidden of the Holy Ghost to preach the word in Asia, after they were come to Mysia, they assayed to go into Bithynia: BUT THE SPIRIT *suffered them not (Acts 16:6, 7).*

God guides His own by closed doors as well as by doors that are wide open. With the best of intentions we may decide upon a certain course of action, then find that the way is blocked before us. Thus far we have known the Lord's unfailing guidance. Does the roadblock mean that we should go some other way, or are we to leap over it in self-assertiveness and self-confidence? Like Paul and Silas, we know that we have been sent forth by a definiteness of guidance that we can never doubt; we know what it means to have the Lord's presence with us and His unfailing provision by the way. Thus far we have walked softly before Him and have always sought His guidance at every turn in the road; but now we cannot go one step farther.

Who is hindering our onward march? Is this what Paul meant in I Thessalonians 2:18, when he wrote, "Wherefore we would have come unto you, even I Paul, once and again; but Satan hindered us"? Or is it the gentle yet insistent hindrance of the Holy Spirit?

There is need for discernment to decide the difference between these two possibilities. We are to resist the enemy and refuse his hindrance. Despite his fierce opposition, we are to press forward with confidence in the promise given in James 4:7 — "Resist the devil, and he will flee from you."

Like Christian in Bunyan's *Pilgrim's Progress,* we are to use the Scriptures, which are the "sword of the Spirit," and the weapon of "all-prayer" (Ephesians 6:17, 18), and thus find triumph over the adversary.

The Spirit we are to obey, for He knows which way we should take and which we should not follow. By prayer and patience, with tenderness of heart and sensitivity of spirit, we are to seek the will of God with willingness for Him to close any door that we should not enter. Thereafter, sooner or later, we shall know why in His wisdom He closed that door only to open another.

As Paul and Silas journeyed northwestward, they were not allowed by the Holy Spirit to turn to the left into the Province of Asia nor to the right into Bithynia. These areas must have seemed to them to be open doors of opportunity and need; but God's time for them had not come as yet. It was only when the apostles came to the end of their land journey and rested by the shores of the Aegean Sea that there came the clear guidance of the Lord of the harvest that they should go over into Macedonia. Thus the Gospel came to Europe. Otherwise, might *we* have been the heathen and the Gospel brought to us from the Far East?

God's hindrance is one method of His guidance. We think we know best; but God knows better.

THE LOVE OF CHRIST

That ye . . . may be able to comprehend . . . the breadth and length and depth and height; and to know the love of Christ which passeth knowledge — Ephesians 3:17-19.

How broad is His love? Oh, as broad as man's trespass,
As wide as the need of the world can be;
And yet to the need of one soul it can narrow —
He came to the world and He came to me.

How long is His love? Without end or beginning,
Eternal as Christ and His life it must be,
For, to everlasting as from everlasting
He loveth the world and He loveth me.

How deep is His love? Oh, as deep as man's sinning.
As low as that uttermost vileness can be;
In the fathomless gulf of the Father's forsaking
He died for the world and He died for me.

How high is His love? It is high as the heavens,
As high as the throne of His glory must be;
And yet from that height He hath stooped to redeem us —
He *so* loved the world and He *so* loved me.

How great is His love? Oh, it passeth all knowledge,
No man's comprehension its measure can be;
It filleth the world, yet each heart may contain it —
He *so* loves the world and He *so* loves me.

— ANNIE JOHNSON FLINT

23.

BUT GOD COMMENDETH HIS LOVE

For when we were yet without strength, in due time Christ died for the ungodly. For scarcely for a righteous man will one die: yet peradventure for a good man some would even dare to die. BUT GOD *commendeth his love toward us, in that, while we were yet sinners, Christ died for us (Romans 5:6-8).*

The setting of this statement on the love of God is indeed startling. *The Amplified New Testament* brings out the contrast clearly and concisely in its translation: "Now it is an extraordinary thing for one to give his life even for an upright man, though perhaps for a noble and lovable and generous benefactor someone might even dare to die. But God shows and clearly proves His (own) love for us by the fact that while we were still sinners Christ, the Messiah, the Anointed One, died for us."

Men have been known to appreciate the "good" man — the kind, considerate, courteous, generous — and even to sacrifice themselves for a such a person. But did anyone ever desire to die for a cruel and contemptible enemy?

God did just that!

By deliberate choice, by wicked works, by hatred and hatefulness, we were enemies to God. By inexplicably strange logic we called the devil our friend and God our enemy. We preferred the broad way to the narrow, our sinfulness to God's salvation, our own waywardness to His way. We were rebels, and unthinkingly we reveled in our rebellion so as to assert our right to do as we please.

Of necessity, the God of holiness must hate sin; but He does not hate the sinner. We are the "ungodly," the "sinners," whom God has loved so much that He sent His only Son to die for our sins.

The love of God either antagonizes the sinner, or it subdues him. The natural mind does not comprehend love that would die for an enemy, and therefore it downgrades the love of God, despises it, or ignores it altogether. Most of mankind give no thought whatever to the love of God for lost men and women. However, when that love *is* given consideration, even casually, its reality grows upon the soul with a sense of guilt that only the grace of God can remove. When that love is received, one begins to understand what the poet meant when he said:

> There is welcome for the sinner,
> And more graces for the good;
> There is mercy with the Saviour;
> There is healing in His blood.
>
> For the love of God is broader
> Than the measure of man's mind;
> And the heart of the Eternal
> Is most wonderfully kind.

We can love our own, and also the good and the gracious; *but God* loves the ungodly, the worst of sinners and the most bitter blasphemers. Our part is to accept that love in His Son, our Savior.

"He That Believeth"

He that believeth shall not make haste — Isaiah 28:16
The king's business requireth haste — I Samuel 21:8.

He that believeth shall not make haste
In useless hurry his strength to waste;
Who walks with God can afford to wait,
For he can never arrive too late.

He that believeth shall not delay;
Who carries the word of the King on its way
Keeps pace with the Pleiades' marching tune,
And he can never arrive too soon.

He that believeth shall walk serene,
With ordered steppings and leisured mien;
He dwells in the midst of eternities,
And the timeless ages of God are his.

—Annie Johnson Flint

24

BUT GOD'S GIFT

Let not sin therefore reign in your mortal body, that ye should obey it in the lusts thereof. Neither yield ye your members as instruments of unrighteousness unto sin: but yield yourselves unto God, as those that are alive from the dead, and your members as instruments of righteousness unto God. . . . For the wages of sin is death; BUT *the gift of God is eternal life through Jesus Christ our Lord (Romans 6:12, 13, 23).*

The devil drives a hard bargain with the unsuspecting sinner, who has little or no understanding how hardheaded and hardhearted the enemy of mankind is. Satan offers the pleasures of sin with its passions and pride. He offers social status and even financial success, education and acclaim, friends, and a full life — without God. The devil, however, exacts payment in full for all that he offers. The carefree and careless, the sophisticated and self-centered, the worldly-wise and worldling — in a word, the sinner — should read the fine print at the bottom of the contract. It states: "The wages of sin is death."

"He that committeth sin," said the Lord Jesus, "is the servant of sin" (John 8:34). Literally, that one is the "bond slave" of sin. Sin at first can be beguiling, intriguing, interesting, and apparently harmless. There is always the thought that one can leave the pathway of sin that leads downward and rapidly retrace one's steps. Sin, however, insidiously increases its domination over the individual, and the broad way that leads to destruction becomes increasingly steep and slippery. Sin, which at the first was alluring, becomes mocking and even mad when the sinner would seek to escape its bondage and turn to God.

Only the penitent sinner who is saved by grace is fully aware of the dreadful wages of sin. When Bunyan's Pilgrim met Apollyon, he was ordered to go back to the City of Destruction, by the enemy who claimed that Christian was his subject. Declared Pilgrim: "I was indeed born in your dominion, but your service was hard, and your wages such as a man could not live on; for the wages of sin is death. . . ." How true!

"But the gift of God" — His goodness to us apart from any deserving on our part — "is eternal life!" It is a gift to be received, and it cannot be earned. Any thought of our paying anything for it, either by good deeds or religious practices, is an insult to the Savior. It is "not by works of righteousness that we have done, but according to his mercy" that we are saved. We are redeemed, declares I Peter 1:18, 19, "not with corruptible things, as silver and gold, but with the precious blood of Christ, as of a lamb without blemish and without spot."

Every day, in one sense, is "pay day." The wages of sin begin to become increasingly apparent to the unsaved; but the final payment of the wages awaits the judgment of the Great White Throne, declares the Bible in Revelation 20:11-15: "And I saw a great white throne, and him that sat on it, from whose face the earth and the heaven fled away; and there was found no place for them. And I saw the dead, small and great, stand before God; and the books were opened: and another book was opened, which is the book of life: and the dead were judged out of those things which were written in the books, according to their works. And the sea gave up the dead which were in it; and death

106

and hell delivered up the dead which were in them: and they were judged every man according to their works. And death and hell were cast into the lake of fire. This is the second death. And whosoever was not found written in the book of life was cast into the lake of fire."

But the gift of God is eternal life. God's word goes on to say:

> And I saw no temple therein: for the Lord God Almighty and the Lamb are the temple of it. And the city had no need of the sun, neither of the moon, to shine in it: for the glory of God did lighten it, and the Lamb is the light thereof. And the nations of them which are saved shall walk in the light of it: and the kings of the earth do bring their glory and honour into it. And the gates of it shall not be shut at all by day: for there shall be no night there (Revelation 21:22-25).

The wages of sin — second death!

The gift of God — eternal life!

The Answered Prayers

We know not what we should pray for as we ought
— Romans 8:26.

I prayed for strength, and then I lost awhile
    All sense of nearness, human and divine;
The love I leaned on failed and pierced my heart;
    The hands I clung to loosed themselves from mine;
But while I swayed, weak, trembling, and alone,
The everlasting arms upheld my own.

I prayed for light; the sun went down in clouds,
    The moon was darkened by a misty doubt,
The stars of heaven were dimmed by earthly fears,
    But all my little candle flames burned out;
But while I sat in shadow, wrapped in night,
The face of Christ made all the darkness bright.

I prayed for peace, and dreamed of restful ease,
    A slumber drugged from pain, a hushed repose;
Above my head the skies were black with storm,
    And fiercer grew the onslaught of my foes;
But while the battle raged, and wild winds blew,
I heard His voice, and perfect peace I knew.

I thank Thee, Lord, Thou wert too wise to heed
    My feeble prayers, and answer as I sought,
Since these rich gifts Thy bounty has bestowed
    Have brought me more than I had asked or thought.
Giver of good, so answer each request
With Thine own giving, better than my best.

—Annie Johnson Flint

25

BUT GOD HAS CHOSEN THE FOOLISH

For after that in the wisdom of God the world by wisdom knew not God, it pleased God by the foolishness of preaching to save them that believe. . . . Because the foolishness of God is wiser than men; and the weakness of God is stronger than men. For ye see your calling, brethren, how that not many wise men after the flesh, not many mighty, not many noble, are called: BUT GOD *hath chosen the foolish things of the world to confound the wise; and God hath chosen the weak things of the world to confound the things which are mighty; and base things of the world, and things which are despised, hath God chosen, yea, and things which are not, to bring to nought things which are: that no flesh should glory in his presence (I Corinthians 1:21, 25-29).*

In his masterpiece, *The Everlasting Mercy,* John Masefield, the late poet laureate of England, describes the thought of the sinner who begins to desire help from someone:

> But trained men's minds are spread so thin,
> They let all sorts of darkness in;
> Whatever light they find, they doubt it,
> They love not light, just talk about it.

The Most High puts no premium on ignorance. He has endowed mankind with intelligence and with the responsibility to make the greatest possible use thereof. Intellectualism apart from the grace of God and humility of heart can make a person so self-sufficient as to realize no need for God. But God's ways are higher than our ways as

heaven is higher than the earth, and because some do not look to God for His truth, whether it be general revelation of nature or in the special revelation of the Scriptures, they do not discern His ways. Out of wide experience, the apostle Paul observed: "For the preaching of the cross is to them that perish foolishness; but unto us which are saved it is the power of God." Therefore, the Scripture continues: "Where is the wise? where is the scribe? where is the disputer of this world? hath not God made foolish the wisdom of this world?"

"The race is not to the swift," declared the Preacher in Ecclesiastes 9:11, "nor the battle to the strong, neither yet bread to the wise, nor yet riches to men of understanding. . . ." Added the Lord Jesus in His prayer, "I thank thee, O Father, Lord of heaven and earth, because thou hast hid these things from the wise and prudent [the clever, those conceited in their learning], and hast revealed them unto babes . . ." (Matthew 11:25, 26).

It is the poor in spirit (the unassuming, the insignificant) who enter the kingdom of heaven. It is the meek who inherit the earth, the merciful who obtain mercy, the pure in heart who see God, and the peacemakers who are the true children of God.

Some of brilliant intellect have received the Savior in child-like faith and simplicity. Some of earth's mightiest men likewise have become true followers of the meek and lowly Jesus. These are not many in comparison with those who are self-sufficient and self-confident, with no need of a Savior. Therefore the Bible states that not many wise by human standards, not many mighty, not many noble (those who depend upon their status in society because of their family or fortune), *but God* has chosen the insignificant and humanly unimportant who are saved by grace and live by faith in the Son of God.

This is what Robert Browning meant when he wrote:

> All I could never be,
> All men ignored in me,
> That I was worth to God.

The Place of Prayer

The place of prayer is a humble place
And ere we enter there
We must leave outside our garb of pride
And our load of worldly care.

The place of prayer is a quiet place.
And at the outer gate
The voice of our will we must firmly still,
And bid our wishes wait.

The place of prayer is a holy place,
And ere we step therein,
With unshod feet our God to meet,
We must put away our sin.

But the place of prayer is high enough
To bring heaven's glory nigh,
And our need speaks clear to our Father's ear,
And is open to His eye.

And the place of prayer is wide enough
For Christ to enter there;
And the humble heart need not depart
Without that vision fair.

And the place of prayer is large enough
To hold God's riches stored,
And faith is the key of the treasury
That opens the secret hoard.

—ANNIE JOHNSON FLINT

26.

BUT GOD HAS REVEALED THEM

And my speech and my preaching was not with en-
ticing words of man's wisdom, but in demonstration of the
Spirit and of power: that your faith should not stand in the
wisdom of men, but in the power of God. Howbeit we
speak wisdom among them that are perfect: yet not the
wisdom of this world, nor of the princes of this world, that
come to nought. . . . But as it is written, Eye hath not seen,
nor ear heard, neither have entered into the heart of man,
the things which God hath prepared for them that love him.
But God hath revealed them unto us by his Spirit: for the
Spirit searcheth all things, yea, the deep things of God
(I Corinthians 2:4-6, 9, 10).

Revelation means God's disclosure or manifestation of
Himself or of His will to mankind, whereby we come to
understand that which we could not achieve by human
study and reflection. To the patriarch, Job, was given the
searching question: "Canst thou by searching find out
God? Canst thou find out the Almighty unto perfection"
(11:7)? The answer is obviously, "No." We human beings,
the most earnest and intelligent of us, are finite and therefore cannot comprehend the Infinite One to perfection.
We see His handiwork in His universe and learn something
of the laws which He has given for the maintenance of
His creation. We accumulate knowledge and by reason
we seek to differentiate truth from error; but our research
and reasoning are subject to human finiteness.

The Bible declares that "Eye hath not seen, nor ear

113

heard, neither have entered into the heart of man, the things which God hath prepared for them that love him; but God hath revealed them unto us by his spirit. . . ." What research cannot reveal and what reason cannot realize can be ours by revelation given to the trusting child of God by the Holy Spirit.

Of Him, the Lord Jesus said to the disciples in the upper room on that last night together: "I have yet many things to say unto you, but ye cannot bear them now. Howbeit when he, the Spirit of truth, is come, he will guide you into all truth; for he shall not speak of himself; but whatsoever he shall hear, that shall he speak: and he will shew you things to come" (John 16:12, 13).

The Almighty has given to us the universe, which is His *general* revelation. By meticulous and reverent study we can learn much of its meaning and therefore appreciate increasingly its Creator. The Bible is God's *special* revelation, given to us by the inspiration of the Holy Spirit and preserved for us all down the generations since first it was given to the prophets and apostles. As we look into God's revelation we realize that despite all the help of microscope and telescope there is the Beyond in the infinite immensity of creation. As we ponder God's Word and believe it, we realize likewise that there is much beyond our understanding; and therefore we look to the Author Himself to teach us. What we cannot perceive, God can and does reveal to us.

By observation and reason we could not find the Almighty; *but God* has revealed Himself in His Word, His Works, and His Son our Savior the Lord Jesus.

GREATER THAN OUR HEARTS

My heart is heavy, my heart is sad,
And clouds have shadowed the joy I had,
Perplexed and doubting, my way I take;
Hast Thou forgotten? Canst Thou forsake?
    Thou — greater than ever my heart can be,
    For my fainting heart give Thy strength to me!

My heart is troubled and tossed within,
Tired of thinking what might have been,
Tired of facing the future years,
Tired of fighting with coward fears;
    Thou — greater than ever my heart can be,
    For my weary heart give Thy rest to me!

My heart is fretted and anxious, too,
Eager to venture and quick to do,
Chafed by inaction, impatient still
At waiting in silence Thy quiet will;
    Thou — greater than ever my heart can be,
    For my restless heart give Thy peace to me!

My heart is empty, my heart is lone,
In the silence of night it maketh moan:
Two walked together, but one is gone,
No footstep echoes beside my own;
    Thou — greater than ever my heart can be,
    For my lonely heart give Thy love to me!

My heart is burdened, my heart is sore,
As manifold sins it counteth o'er;
I long to be holy, Thou Holy One,
But swift to do evil my feet will run;
    Thou — greater than ever my heart can be,
    For my sinful heart give Thyself to me!

— ANNIE JOHNSON FLINT

27

BUT GOD GAVE THE INCREASE

I have planted, Apollos watered; but God gave the increase. So then neither is he that planteth any thing, neither he that watereth; BUT GOD *that giveth the increase (I Corinthians 3:6, 7).*

There is the natural inclination of our hearts to want credit for all that we do. We covet the approval and applause of our fellow men, and are encouraged thereby. That subtle self-centeredness steals its way into our service for God, and can be very damaging, even destructive, to its true effectiveness.

Every Christian is to be a witness for his Savior. Just before His ascension into heaven the Lord Jesus said to His disciples, "Ye shall receive power, after that the Holy Spirit is come upon you; and ye shall be witnesses unto me both in Jerusalem, and in all Judaea, and in Samaria, and unto the uttermost parts of the earth" (Acts 1:8). Such witnessing for our Lord after what He has done for us brings others to a sense of need and leads them to the saving grace of God.

To each believer is given at least one gift of the Holy Spirit. Declares I Corinthians 12:6-8, 11: "And there are diversities of operations, but it is the same God which worketh all in all. But the manifestation of the Spirit is given to every man to profit withal [that is, to use the gift effectively and faithfully]. For to one is given by the Spirit the word of wisdom; to another the word of knowledge by the same Spirit . . . but all these worketh that one and the selfsame Spirit, dividing to every man severally as he will."

In God's work there is team work; we are "labourers together with God" (v. 9) and also one with another. None is to say, "This *I* have done!" Rather, the word should be, "This *we* have done!" Those early Corinthians were inclined, like twentieth century believers, to be attached to some one servant of God. Some were "of Paul" and others were "of Apollos," who had been very effective in evangelism and Bible teaching in their midst. They needed to be reminded that it was "God [who] gave the increase." For a harvest there may be one who plows and cultivates the soil, another who sows the seed, and still another who does the reaping. The last named did not do it all. For the harvest, God's sunshine and rain are indispensable.

The late D. L. Moody was asked how many seekers had been dealt with by Christian witnesses before accepting the Savior in a campaign. "At least ninety-five percent," was his astonishing reply. Many Christians had entered into the Lord's work by witnessing to neighbors and relatives; the end result was their conversion at a Moody and Sankey campaign. Billy Graham and the Team are finding the same situation in our day in the evangelistic crusades on every continent.

Each of us has responsibility for the work committed to us, whether it be public or private, conspicuous or wholly inconspicuous. As each one does his part, then God will give the increase. The secret of true growth in the Lord's work is simply this: One sows the Word, another waters the same with prayer and tears, *but God* gives the increase.

GREAT GRACE

His grace is great enough to meet the great things,
　　The crashing waves that overwhelm the soul,
The roaring winds that leave us stunned and breathless,
　　The sudden storms beyond our life's control.
His grace is great enough to meet the small things,
　　The little pin-prick troubles that annoy,
The insect worries, buzzing and persistent,
　　The squeaking wheels that grate upon our joy.

　　　　　　　　　— ANNIE JOHNSON FLINT

28

BUT GOD IS ABLE

Wherefore let him that thinketh he standeth take heed lest he fall. There hath no temptation taken you but such as is common to man: BUT GOD *is faithful, who will not suffer you to be tempted above that ye are able; but will with the temptation also make a way to escape, that ye may be able to bear it (I Corinthians 10:12, 13).*

We are sometimes tempted to believe that our trials and perplexities are peculiar to *us* and that they constitute complications unfamiliar to anyone else. Such is not the case, and the *Amplified* translation of I Corinthians 10:13 states it emphatically and accurately: "For no temptation — no trial regarded as enticing to sin [no matter how it comes or where it leads] — has overtaken you *and* laid hold on you that is not common to man — that is, no temptation or trial has come to you that is beyond human resistance and that is not adjusted and adapted and belonging to human experience, and such as man can bear. But God is faithful [to His Word and to His compassionate nature], and He [can be trusted] not to let you be tempted *and* tried *and* assayed beyond your ability *and* strength of resistance *and* power to endure, but with the temptation He will [always] also provide the way out — the means of escape to a landing place — that you may be capable *and* strong *and* powerful patiently to bear up under it." The temptation is the testing of our faith and patience, and is the setting in which we find the faithfulness of God.

None of us is exempt from difficulties and dilemmas.

For some the distress goes deeper than for others. The trial comes more suddenly and lasts longer for some than for others. When the perplexity and the pain persist, we reason that they are unnecessary and undeserved. They may seem wholly meaningless, and to all appearances endless.

There is a limit to human endurance. We may not be familiar with this frontier, though sometimes we think we have passed beyond it. Like the apostle Paul, we call earnestly upon God for deliverance; but no help seems to come. Only then did he learn the truth, shared by grateful fellow Christians all down the ages, that God's grace is sufficient for every circumstance and that His strength is made perfect in our weakness (II Corinthians 12:9).

God knows the boundary of our bewilderment — that is, the extent to which we can endure. This promise assures us: "But God is faithful, who will not suffer you to be tempted above that ye are able: but will with the temptation also make a way to escape, that ye may be able to bear it." Note that the faithfulness of God is available to us *during* the time of testing and not after it has passed away. It is *with* the temptation that He makes a way to escape. It is *"in* the darkness" that light arises (Psalm 112:4). It is *"in* all these things" (tribulation, distress, persecution, danger) that we are "more than conquerors through him that loved us" (Romans 8:37).

We are to look steadfastly to the Faithful One for His help, and not to a change of circumstances. In His time and in His way He delivers His own. He is never too late, nor does He come with help that is too little. Conditions may deteriorate, misunderstandings and misrepresentation may increase, friends may grow fainthearted or fail; *but God* "is faithful to His word and to His compassionate nature, and He can be trusted not to let you be tempted . . . beyond your ability of resistance and power to endure." With the prophet Habakkuk we can declare with confidence: "Although the fig tree shall not blossom, neither shall fruit be in the vines; the labour of the olive shall fail, and the fields shall yield no meat; the flock shall be cut off from the fold, and there shall be no herd in the stalls: yet I will rejoice in the Lord, I will joy in the God of my salvation" (Habakkuk 3:17, 18).

The New Tomb

*And he took the body of Jesus and laid it
in a new tomb — Matthew 27:60.*

There is no new sorrow!
    Ancient as the race
Are the woes that pierce us,
    Old and commonplace:
But to each heart stricken
    All the ages through,
Grief is never ancient,
    Every tomb is "new."

There is no new comfort!
    Old as truth and tears
Comes the tender message
    Floating down the years;
To each sad heart mourning
    By its own new tomb
Sound the angel voices
    From the shadowy gloom:

"Lo! your dead are living,
    And they walk in light
Where there comes no weeping,
    Where there falls no night;
Where, by crystal waters,
    Fadeless flowers bloom; —
Into God's fair garden
    Opens this new tomb."
            — Annie Johnson Flint

29

BUT NOW IS CHRIST RISEN

For if the dead rise not, then is not Christ raised: and if Christ be not raised, your faith is vain; ye are yet in your sins. Then they also which are fallen asleep in Christ are perished. If in this life only we have hope in Christ, we are of all men most miserable. But now is Christ risen from the dead, and become the firstfruits of them that slept (I Corinthians 15:16-20).

If the Lord Jesus Christ be not risen from the dead, then what?

The Bible faces that question: "If the dead rise not, then is not Christ raised; and if Christ be not raised. . . ."

If Christ be not raised from the dead, then the gospel account is untrue, the Bible contains falsehoods, and there is no Christian message. Then we have no basis for any Christian faith. Those who wrote the four gospels and those who have proclaimed the resurrection are "false witnesses of God" (v. 15). They were deceivers and we have been deceived.

If Christ be not raised, He would never have been remembered; or at most we might have had fragmentary reference to an itinerant Galilean teacher who was executed because of his criticism of the religious status quo of his day. We might possibly have some ethical teaching from him; but there is the possibility that no one would have taken the trouble to write down, for example, *the Sermon on the Mount,* after Jesus of Nazareth had been crucified on Calvary's hillside and buried in Joseph's tomb. If Christ was not raised, we have no Savior from the penalty and power of indwelling sin and those who died believing in him have perished forever. The Scripture states that truth succinctly: "And if Christ be not raised, your faith is vain; ye are yet in your sins" (v. 17).

The Corinthian Christians to whom this word was first sent, as written by the apostle Paul under the inspiration of the Holy Spirit, knew that they were no longer under the domination and condemnation of sin. In responding to the gospel invitation they had turned from their sinful and shameful past and had become new men and women in the Savior. They knew that Paul wrote accurately of them when he declared: "Be not deceived: neither fornicators, nor idolaters, nor adulterers, nor effeminate, nor abusers of themselves with mankind, nor thieves, nor covetous, nor drunkards, nor revilers, nor extortioners, shall inherit the kingdom of God. And such were some of you: but ye are washed, but ye are sanctified, but ye are justified in the name of the Lord Jesus, and by the Spirit of our God" (I Corinthians 6:9-11). They had been forgiven, cleansed, declared righteous in the righteousness of Christ, and they knew true holiness by the indwelling Holy Spirit. They knew that their faith was not something empty and meaningless. They were no longer in sin, because Christ had been raised from the dead after having paid the penalty for sin in His death on Calvary's cross.

If Christ be not raised, a funeral would be a most hopeless and fearful occasion. No song, only the death wail of the heathen; no assurance of everlasting life, only the darkness and dread of the grave. Such would be our situation.

But because He who is the Resurrection and the Life lives, every believer in Him will live with Him beyond the grave. He is the "firstfruits," and we the harvest at His coming again!

THE LOST VOICES

Northward again the happy birds, returning,
    Shall sing for us the songs we thought were lost;
They were but waiting in a fairer country,
    Untouched by storm and frost.

And when the lonely winter of our sorrow
    Has rounded out for us Earth's changing year,
Oh, on some radiant morn what long-hushed voices
    Shall greet our listening ear!

— ANNIE JOHNSON FLINT

30.

BUT GOD GIVES IT A BODY

But some man will say, How are the dead raised up?
and with what body do they come? Thou fool, that which
thou sowest is not quickened, except it die: and that which
thou sowest, thou sowest not that body that shall be, but
bare grain, it may chance of wheat, or of some other grain:
BUT GOD *giveth it a body as it hath pleased him, and to*
every seed his own body (I Corinthians 15:35-38).

"If a man die, shall he live again?" is one of the oldest
queries of the human heart. Job asked that question (14:14)
after making the observation: "For there is hope of a tree,
if it be cut down, that it will sprout again, and that the
tender branch thereof will not cease. Though the root thereof wax old in the earth, and the stock thereof die in the
ground; yet through the scent of water it will bud, and
bring forth boughs like a plant. But man dieth, and wasteth
away: yea, man giveth up the ghost, and where is he"
(14:7-10)?

The reality of the resurrection and life after death have
been made perfectly clear and convincing by the resurrection of the Savior. Declares I Corinthians 15:20: "But now
is Christ risen from the dead, and become the firstfruits of
them that slept." Granted that assurance, there is still the
understandable inquisitiveness of the human heart to peer
into the future and to inquire, "How are the dead raised
up, and with what body do they come?" The Scriptural answer is couched in botanical language. The body is likened
to seed sown in a field. Obviously the plant which arises out
of the death of that seed is vitally related to it, but unlike

129

it in appearance. Furthermore, each seed produces after its own kind; therefore, we can distinguish wheat from barley, corn from cotton, petunias from pansies, and so on. All the fruitfulness of grain and the loveliness and fragrance of flowers are contained in the tiny seed which is totally dissimilar in appearance to that which grows up.

Thus is the resurrection of the dead. In the vivid translation of *The Amplified New Testament*, I Corinthians 15:42-44, reads: "So it is with the resurrection of the dead. [The body] that is sown is perishable and decays, but [the body] that is resurrected is imperishable — immune to decay, immortal. [Dan. 12:3.] It is sown in dishonor and humiliation; it is raised in honor and glory. It is sown in infirmity and weakness; it is resurrected in strength and endued with power. It is sown a natural (physical) body; it is raised a supernatural (a spiritual) body. [As surely as] there is a physical body, there is also a spiritual body."

The physical body is adapted to the environment of this life. The spiritual body is a body, to be sure, but it is adapted to the life of the spirit as well as to physical life. The only indication we have of it is the body of the resurrected Savior who walked with two friends to Emmaus, who came into a room when all doors were locked, who ate fish and honey with them, and who ascended bodily into heaven.

Now we know only in part, and we desire to know fully what our resurrection body will be. Like a grain of wheat, the physical body is sown in death. *"But God* giveth it a body as it hath pleased him, and to every seed his own body"!

130

At the Place of the Sea

By the greatness of thine arm they shall be still . . . till
thy people pass over, O Lord — Exodus 15:16.

Have you come to the Red Sea place in your life,
    Where, in spite of all you can do,
There is no way out, there is no way back,
    There is no other way but — through?
Then wait on the Lord with a trust serene
    Till the night of your fear is gone;
He will send the wind, He will heap the floods,
    When He says to your soul, "Go on."

And His hand will lead you through — clear through —
    Ere the watery walls roll down,
No foe can reach you, no wave can touch,
    No mightiest sea can drown;
The tossing billows may rear their crests,
    Their foam at your feet may break,
But over their bed you shall walk dry shod
    In the path that your Lord will make.

In the morning watch, 'neath the lifted cloud,
    You shall see but the Lord alone,
When He leads you on from the place of the sea
    To land that you have not known;
And your fears shall pass as your foes have passed,
    You shall be no more afraid;
You shall sing His praise in a better place,
    A place that His hand has made.

                  — Annie Johnson Flint

31.

BUT GOD IS RICH IN MERCY

And you hath he quickened, who were dead in trespasses and sins: wherein in time past ye walked according to the course of this world, according to the prince of the power of the air, the spirit that now worketh in the children of disobedience: among whom also we all had our conversation in times past in the lusts of our flesh, fulfilling the desires of the flesh and of the mind; and were by nature the children of wrath, even as others. BUT GOD, who is rich in mercy, for his great love wherewith he loved us, even when we were dead in sins, hath quickened us together with Christ, (by grace ye are saved;) (Ephesians 2:1-5).

The Scriptures make frequent reference to the spiritual wealth available to God's people. The Bible speaks of "the riches of his goodness" (Romans 2:4), which theologians call "common grace." It also makes reference to "the riches of the glory of his inheritance in the saints" (Ephesians 1:18; 3:16) made known to us by the indwelling Holy Spirit. Then there are the "riches of his grace," which tell of "redemption through his blood, the forgiveness of sins" (Ephesians 1:7). In Ephesians 2:4 are the riches of His mercy.

Our spiritual poverty, apart from the riches of God's mercy and love, quite beggars description. This Scripture declares that we were "dead in trespasses and sins" and under the "prince of the power of the air, the spirit that now worketh in the children of disobedience."

Our lost condition is described vividly throughout the Bible. The prophet Isaiah observed: "All we like sheep have

133

gone astray; we have turned every one to his own way" and then adds the prophetic words regarding the Savior's death on Calvary's cross seven hundred years later, "and the Lord hath laid on him the iniquity of us all" (53:6). The Lord Jesus taught so plainly that "God sent not his Son into the world to condemn the world; but that the world through him might be saved. He that believeth on him is not condemned: but he that believeth not is condemned already, because he hath not believed in the name of the only begotten Son of God. And this is the condemnation, that light is come into the world, and men loved darkness rather than light, because their deeds were evil. For every one that doeth evil hateth the light, neither cometh to the light, lest his deeds should be reproved. But he that doeth truth cometh to the light, that his deeds may be made manifest, that they are wrought in God" (John 3:17-21).

We are by nature the children of wrath, even as others — but God. . . !

The Amplified New Testament is very graphic in this Scripture: "But God! So rich is He in His mercy! Because of and in order to satisfy the great and wonderful and intense love with which He loved us. . . ."

We had no way in which to escape the bondage of the devil or to rise out of spiritual death into the life of God; *but God* could do that and has done it for every true believer in the Savior. It is of God's mercy that we were not destroyed when we were in sin, or that we were not left to our own devices. In compassion He sent His only Son, the Lord Jesus Christ, the great Shepherd of the sheep to give His life so that we might live in Him.

When Bunyan's penitent Pilgrim came to the cross, his heavy burden of sin "loosed from off his shoulders, and fell from off his back, and began to tumble, and so continued to do till it came to the mouth of the sepulchre, where it fell in, and I saw it no more." To him came with assurance that word from the Savior, "Thy sins be forgiven thee." Observed Bunyan: "Then Christian gave three leaps for joy, and went on singing,

> Thus far did I come laden with my sin,
> Nor could aught ease the grief that I was in,
> Till I came hither. What a place is this!
> Must here be the beginning of my bliss?
> Must here the burden fall from off my back?
> Must here the strings that bound it to me crack?
> Blest cross! blest sepulchre! blest, rather, be
> The Man that there was put to shame for me!

Lost in sin; *but God* who is rich in mercy?

Under sin's condemnation; but by grace we are saved.

WHEN CHRIST WAITS

If any man . . . open the door, I will come in
— Revelation 3:20.

What a wonderful thing is this
That man may choose as he will
To open the door and let Christ in,
Or make Him wait at the sill!

The sovereign Lord of the universe,
Courteous, stands and knocks;
He will not batter the shut door down,
Nor break the bolts and locks.

For man has the power of choice,
He can lift the latch if he will;
There is no knob on the outer side,
And the Lord Christ waits at the sill.

He patiently knocks and patiently waits
For man to open the door;
Beware the day when His patience ends,
And the pierced Hand knocks no more!

— ANNIE JOHNSON FLINT

32

BUT GOD HAD MERCY ON HIM

But I trust in the Lord that I also myself shall come shortly. Yet I supposed it necessary to send to you Epaphroditus, my brother, and companion in labour, and fellow-soldier, but your messenger, and he that ministered to my wants. For he longed after you all, and was full of heaviness, because that ye had heard that he had been sick. For indeed he was sick nigh unto death: BUT GOD *had mercy on him; and not on him only, but on me also, lest I should have sorrow upon sorrow (Philippians 2:24-27).*

The mercy of God is measureless. Psalm 103:11 declares: "As the heaven is high above the earth, so great is his mercy toward them that fear him." The height of heaven, who can measure it? Beyond the clouds and the atmosphere of our little earth, beyond the relatively nearby moon and the sun (merely 93,000,000 miles away!), beyond the farthest galaxy in the heavens, so great is God's mercy.

Some concept of the immensity of divine compassion was learned by Jeremiah the prophet in the dark days of Jerusalem's decline and captivity. He could say: "It is of the Lord's mercies that we are not consumed, because his compassions fail not. They are new every morning; great is thy faithfulness" (Lamentations 3:22, 23).

God has a way of showing His mercy toward us through the life of another. Epaphroditus was very dear to the apostle Paul, who spoke of him as "my brother, and companion in labour, and fellow soldier." He had come from Philippi to help care for the aged missionary. There he was taken ill and obviously human hope for him was largely lost, because he was "nigh unto death." "*But God* had mercy on him," says Paul, "and not on him only, but on me also." In answer to prayer, Epaphroditus was restored to health and continued to be a joy to the imprisoned apostle and to his hometown fellow believers in Philippi.

It was much the same experience Paul had earlier, as recorded in II Corinthians 7:5-7. Of that trial he wrote: "For, when we were come into Macedonia, our flesh had no rest, but we were troubled on every side; without were fightings, within were fears. *Nevertheless God,* that comforteth those that are cast down, comforted us by the coming of Titus. . . ."

How will God show His mercy to us today? He will do so in His Word as we read it and appropriate it to ourselves. He may show it through a letter from a friend or stranger, or someone near at hand or far away. Or He may use us to show His mercy to some child of His who is in difficulty, darkness, or despair. That mercy is still as high as heaven is above the earth on behalf of His trusting people.

Trouble on every side; nevertheless God!

Nigh unto death; but God had mercy!

COUNTED WORTHY

Rejoicing that they were counted worthy to suffer
— Acts 5:41.

If so be that we suffer with him, that we may be also
glorified together — Romans 8:17.

This weighty burden thou dost bear,
    This heavy cross,
It is a gift the Lord bestows,
    And not a loss;
It is a trust that He commits
    Unto thy care,
A precious lesson He has deigned
    With thee to share.
Rejoice that He so honors thee
    And so esteems,
That He should give into thy hands
    The things He deems
Of highest worth; the crown of thorns
    With Him to wear,
And all the suffering of that crown
    With Him to bear,
That by and by His glory, too,
    With Him thou'lt share.

                — ANNIE JOHNSON FLINT

33.

BUT GOD SHALL SUPPLY

But I rejoiced in the Lord greatly, that now at the last your care of me hath flourished again; wherein ye were also careful, but ye lacked opportunity. Not that I speak in respect of want: for I have learned, in whatsoever state I am, therewith to be content. I know both how to be abased, and I know how to abound: every where and in all things I am instructed both to be full and to be hungry, both to abound and to suffer need. I can do all things through Christ which strengtheneth me. . . . But I have all, and abound: I am full, having received of Epaphroditus the things which were sent from you, an odour of a sweet smell, a sacrifice acceptable, wellpleasing to God. BUT MY GOD shall supply all your need according to his riches in glory by Christ Jesus (Philippians 4:10-13, 18, 19).

"Godliness with contentment is great gain," declare the Scriptures. The *Amplified* version reads: ". . . godliness accompanied with contentment — that contentment which is a sense of inward sufficiency — is great and abundant gain" (I Timothy 6:6). The contented heart within the Christian is not dependent upon outward circumstances for its confidence and courage. Like the apostle Paul, that heart can say: "I was made very happy in the Lord that now you have revived your interest in my welfare after so long a time; you were indeed thinking of me, but you had no opportunity to show it. Not that I am implying that I was in any personal want, for I have learned how to be content (satisfied to the point where I am not disturbed or disquieted) in whatever state I am. I know how to be abased and live humbly in

straitened circumstances, and I know also how to enjoy plenty and live in abundance. I have learned in any and all circumstances, the secret of facing every situation, whether well-fed or going hungry, having a sufficiency and to spare or going without and being in want" (Philippians 4:10-12, *The Amplified New Testament*).

This invaluable lesson of being content in poverty or prosperity, in sickness or health, in darkness or delight, can be learned only by experience, as stated in Romans 5:3-5: ". . . tribulation worketh patience; and patience, experience; and experience, hope: and hope maketh not ashamed: because the love of God is shed abroad in our hearts by the Holy Ghost which is given unto us." The humbled, unhurried heart has learned the lesson: "I can do all things through Christ which strengtheneth me."

Because of our deep and increasing acquaintance with our Lord, we can assure others that He will likewise supply all their need. Not infrequently we find that our efforts to encourage and strengthen others by spiritual and material help is answered by ingratitude or indifference, and even possibly by insufficiency for our own necessities. Such was not the case with the apostle Paul, because he was deeply grateful for all that the Philippian believers had done for him. They needed the confidence, however, that God would make provision for all their need. Such supply would be in proportion to God's inexhaustible resources, and not out of them, as we are inclined to read this promise. The word is *according to*. The Most High is not impoverished by His giving to us all that we need. Therefore, when every human resource and recourse fail, however well intentioned they may be, the heart is to have this assurance: *"But my God shall supply. . . !"*

He will!

For All the Morrows

Has the year brought sadness?
　　Joy is yet in store.
Has it given gladness?
　　Next year giveth more.
Let your Father measure
　　All your pain and care,
Let Him weigh the burden
　　That your heart must bear,
Sending light or shadow
　　As He deemeth best,
For in His sure wisdom
　　You can safely rest.
Peace for all the morrows,
　　Strength for all the days,
These shall be your portion
　　Through the New Year's ways.

— ANNIE JOHNSON FLINT

34.

BUT GOD IS FAITHFUL

Finally, brethren, pray for us, that the word of the Lord may have free course, and be glorified, even as it is with you: and that we may be delivered from unreasonable and wicked men: for all men have not faith. BUT THE LORD *is faithful, who shall stablish you, and keep you from evil (II Thessalonians 3:1-3).*

God's faithfulness has ever been strength and solace to tested believers. In the midst of utter human loneliness and loss, in darkness and human despair, Jeremiah wrote the Lamentations. While remembering his many afflictions and misery, he could say, "My soul hath them still in remembrance, and is humbled in me. This I recall to my mind, therefore have I hope. It is of the Lord's mercies that we are not consumed, because his compassions fail not. They are new every morning: great is thy faithfulness. The Lord is my portion, saith my soul; therefore will I hope in him. The Lord is good unto them that wait for him, to the soul that seeketh him" (Lamentations 3:20-25). God's faithfulness is written large throughout the Scriptures. The Psalms abound in references to that divine attribute; for example, we read: "Mercy shall be built up forever: thy faithfulness shalt thou establish in the very heavens." And therefore with assurance the psalmist says: "O Lord God of hosts, who is a strong Lord like unto thee? or to thy faithfulness round about thee" (89:2, 8)? We are to count upon that faithfulness because God suffers it not to fail.

The apostle Paul requested that the Thessalonian Christians pray for the evangelists, Silas, Timothy, and Paul himself. The first petition was that "the word of the Lord may have free course, and be glorified" (II Thessalonians 3:1). The cause of the Gospel was uppermost in his desire. He knew that the entrance of God's Word would bring light to those who sat in darkness and the shadow of death. He had learned that the Word is like a sharp sword that enters deeply into the sinful heart and brings it under conviction. By the Word of God young believers were being built up. Therefore the request that the Word of God should run swiftly and have its effectiveness.

Then there was the further request "that we may be delivered from unreasonable and wicked men; for all men have not faith" (v. 2). Paul had learned that "if any live godly in Christ Jesus he will suffer persecution," as he later wrote to Timothy. Satan seeks to use wicked men to prevent the preaching of the Gospel and to undo, if possible, the work that has been done. Therefore there was this petition for deliverance from those who hate God and the Gospel of the Lord Jesus Christ.

Men can be cruel and cunning against Christians, especially against young believers, as were these Thessalonians. That is still true today wherever the Gospel goes forth. Our Christian brethren behind the walls of iron and bamboo or in lands where superstition and idolatry prevail know what it means to be persecuted for righteousness' sake and to be hated, even killed, because of their godly life and consistent testimony. For them as well as for ourselves there should be this confidence: *But the Lord* is faithful! He is faithful to establish his own in the faith, and faithful to keep them from evil men and the evil one.

THE INTERCESSOR

Christ . . . who also maketh intercession for us
— Romans 8:34.

Infinite Wisdom and infinite Love,
Praying for me to the Father above,
Asking for me what Thou knowest is best —
Surely my heart in this knowledge can rest.
Wrapped in my darkness and ignorance here,
With Thy great prayer let me not interfere;
Let me not cross that petition divine,
Losing a blessing that might have been mine;
Teach me to pray, that Thy will, so begun,
May in my life and my spirit be done.
Here is my confidence, here can I rest;
Thou alone knowest and askest the best.

— ANNIE JOHNSON FLINT

35

BUT GOD THE SON HAS AN UNCHANGEABLE PRIESTHOOD

And they truly were many priests, because they were not suffered to continue by reason of death: BUT *this man, because he continueth ever, hath an unchangeable priesthood. Wherefore he is able also to save them to the uttermost that come unto God by him, seeing he ever liveth to make intercession for them. For such an high priest became us, who is holy, harmless, undefiled, separate from sinners, and made higher than the heavens; who needeth not daily, as those high priests, to offer up sacrifice, first for his own sins, and then for the people's: for this he did once, when he offered up himself (Hebrews 7:23-27).*

Priesthood is God's provision for the spiritual welfare of mankind. The Bible teaches that in the original creation man was constituted prophet, priest, and king, with responsibilities and duties in each area of his life. The father was to be. the teacher of God's truth to his own household, and the one to intercede in their behalf. That we read of Abraham, for example, or of Job who prayed daily for all his children.

When the Israelites were led out of Egypt and received the law at Mount Sinai in the desert, the priesthood of the family of Levi was established. For that priesthood there was a "Holy Place" in the Tabernacle where sacrifices were offered and prayers were made. The law and the Levitical priesthood were designed to prepare Israel for the coming of the Messiah who would fulfill the sacrifices and ceremonies of the law and would establish a new priesthood.

With the passing of the Old Covenant, in which there was the Levitical priesthood, there came the New Covenant established in the Lord Jesus Christ. He Himself is now our Great High Priest. Hebrews 4:14-16 plainly sets forth this truth: "Seeing then that we have a great high priest, that is passed into the heavens, Jesus the Son of God, let us hold fast our profession. For we have not an high priest which cannot be touched with the feeling of our infirmities; but was in all points tempted like as we are, yet without sin. Let us therefore come boldly unto the throne of grace, that we may obtain mercy, and find grace to help in time of need."

With our Great High Priest now in the heavens there is no longer a special order of priests; rather, every believer is a priest of God. We read in I Peter 2:9, "Ye are a chosen generation, a royal priesthood, an holy nation, a peculiar people; that ye should shew forth the praises of him who hath called you out of darkness into his marvellous light."

The priesthood of the Old Covenant changed frequently in its personnel because of death. The contrast in this statement, "But this man, because he continueth ever, hath an unchangeable priesthood" (Hebrews 7:24) is to make evident that Jesus Christ "is able also to save them to the uttermost that come unto God by him, seeing he ever liveth to make intercession for them" (v. 25).

Because of our Great High Priest and His salvation, each believer has access to the throne of God by the "new and living way." Therefore, we have the exhortation, "Let us draw near with a true heart in full assurance of faith, having our hearts sprinkled from an evil conscience, and our bodies washed with pure water. Let us hold fast the profession of our faith, without wavering; (for he is faithful that promised)" (Hebrews 10:20-23).

The Old Testament priesthood passed away: *but* the High Priest of the New Testament age is our Savior, now at the right hand of God the Father, and coming soon to be King over all the earth.

His Billows

All thy . . . billows are gone over me — Psalm 42:7.

They are His billows, whether they go over us
  Hiding His face in smothering spray and foam,
Or, smooth and sparkling, spread a path before us,
  And to our haven bear us safely home.

They are His billows, whether, for our succour,
  He walks across them, stilling all our fear,
Or to our cry there comes nor aid nor answer,
  And in the lonely silence none is near.

They are His billows, whether we are toiling
  Through tempest-driven waves that never cease,
While deep to deep with clamor loud is calling,
  Or at His word they hush themselves in peace.

They are His billows, whether He divides them,
  Making us walk dry shod where seas had flowed,
Or lets tumultuous breakers surge about us
  Rushing unchecked across our only road.

They are His billows, and He brings us through them;
  So has He promised, so His love will do;
Keeping and leading, guiding and upholding,
  To His sure harbor, He will bring us through.

— Annie Johnson Flint

But to summarize:

These lessons by no means exhaust the Biblical emphasis on the truth: *but God.*

We could mention David's desperate situation when pursued by King Saul, who "sought him every day, *but God* delivered him not into his hand" (I Samuel 23:14). The psalmist observed with apprehension the assemblies of violent and vindictive men who desired his destruction; "*but thou,* O Lord, art a God full of compassion . . ." (Psalm 86:15). It is true that "all the gods of the nations are idols: *but the Lord* made the heavens" (Psalm 96:5). "The Lord preserveth the strangers; he relieveth the fatherless and widow: *but* the way of the wicked he turneth upside down" (Psalm 146:9).

In apostolic days there was bitter and brutal persecution against the believers in Christ, "*but* the word of God grew and multiplied" (Acts 12:24). The truly penitent know the pain of conviction because of sin, and then the inexpressible pleasure of knowing sins are forgiven, and can sing with the psalmist (130:3, 4):

If thou, Lord, shouldest mark iniquities,

O Lord, who shall stand? *But* there is for-

giveness with thee, that thou mayest be feared.

Such are born again, "not of blood [that is, by human generation], nor by the will of man, *but of God*" (John 1:13).

❀　❀　❀　❀　❀　❀　❀　❀　❀